ABDOMINAL
TRAINING

CHRISTOPHER M. NORRIS

A & C Black · London

For Hildegard and Sophie

First published 1997 by
A & C Black (Publishers) Ltd
35 Bedford Row, London WC1R 4JH

Reprinted 1999

ISBN 0 7136 4585 7

A CIP catalogue record for this book
is available from the British Library.

Acknowledgements
Cover photograph courtesy of Jump, Hamburg.
Line diagrams by Jean Ashley.

Typeset in Palatino 12/13pt

Printed and bound in Great Britain by
The Lavenham Press, Suffolk

CONTENTS

INTRODUCTION

There are many types of training available today, each with a specific aim. Some aim to reduce weight, others to strengthen muscle, and still others to increase general fitness. Most fashionable abdominal exercise programmes are designed to work the mid-section hard and make the muscles 'hurt', in the belief that this will 'flatten the tummy' or 'trim the waist'. They are normally based on exercise to music classes, or on sport. These programmes often talk about 'going for the burn' and 'pumping up'. Unfortunately, they are not suitable for those of poor or even average fitness levels, firstly because they arc too demanding, and secondly because they place excessive stress on the lower back.

The abdominal programme described in this book is very different. It does not come from a sporting background, but from physiotherapy exercises designed to rehabilitate the spine following injury. As such it aims to be both safe and effective, and to develop trunk fitness which is relevant to everyday life rather than just to sport. In physiotherapy terms, this type of training is called 'functional', hence the term Functional Load Abdominal Training (F.L.A.T.).

How the spine works

Overview of the spinal column

The human backbone, or 'spinal column', is made up of 33 bones. Each bone is called a 'vertebra', and the vertebrae are formed into five groups (*see* fig. 1). In the neck the bones, called 'cervical vertebrae', are delicate but highly mobile, enabling you to turn your head fully. In the chest region the bones are called 'thoracic vertebrae' and these bones connect to the ribs. In the lower spine the spinal bones are called 'lumbar vertebrae'. These are large, strong bones covered with powerful muscles. Below the lumbar vertebrae are the remnants of our tail. The 'sacrum' is a triangular shaped bone which attaches at the sides to the pelvis, while the 'coccyx' forms a thin, pointed tip to the end of the spine.

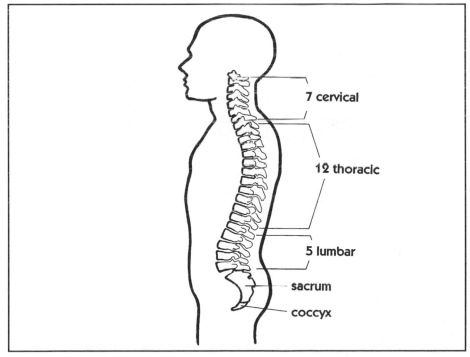

Fig.1 *The spinal column*

SPINAL CURVES ●

Although the spinal vertebrae stand one on top of each other, the column they make is not straight. Instead, the spine forms an 'S' curve. There are two inward curves in the lower back and neck, while the thoracic spine curves gently outwards. These curves are not present at birth, but begin to develop in early childhood.

In the early years of life, a baby's spine is rounded, and we call this rounded shape the 'primary spinal curve' (*see* fig. 2a). As the baby starts to lie on its front and lift its head up, the neck curve starts to form (*see* fig. 2b). It is not until a baby stands up that the curve in the lower back is formed (*see* fig. 2c). Because the neck and lower back curves form later, they are called 'secondary spinal curves'.

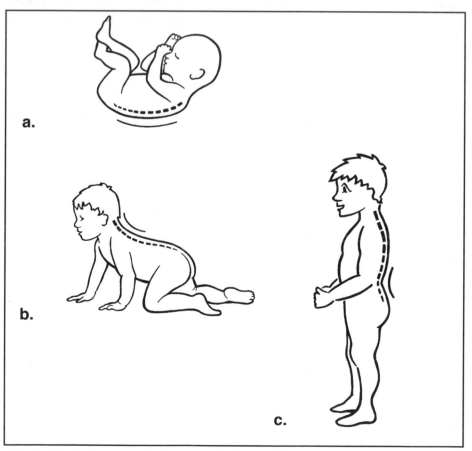

Fig.2 *(a) Primary spinal curve; (b) secondary curve in neck; (c) secondary curve in lower back*

If the spine was completely straight, when we run or jump a large amount of shock would be transmitted up to the head. The function of the spinal curves is to enable the spine to act in a spring-like fashion, absorbing some of the shock of movement and making actions more agile.

When the spinal curves are altered, stress can be placed on the spine. This can occur through alterations in posture and the way we work. Long periods spent sitting at desks and driving a car will change the important curve in the lumbar region and this can be one source of low back pain.

• • • • • • • • • • • • • • • • • **KEYPOINT** • • • • • • • • • • • • • • • • • •

Maintaining a correct curve in the lower back is important to overall spinal health.

THE SPINAL SEGMENT •

Each pair of spinal bones together forms a single unit called a 'spinal segment' (*see* fig. 3). The two bones are separated by a spongy disc attached to the flat part of the bone. At the back of the vertebra the bone is extended to form two small joints called 'facets'. From above it can be seen that the back of the spinal bone forms a hollow arch through which runs the spinal cord carrying messages from the brain to the legs and arms (*see* fig. 4).

Fig.3 The spinal segment

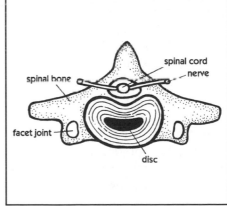

Fig.4 Cross section through the spine

SPINAL LIGAMENTS •

Bending forwards will stretch the ligaments behind the spine but relax those in front. Bending backwards will reverse the situation, stretching the front ligaments but relaxing those covering the back of the spine. If you perform an exercise which persistently overstretches a ligament, the ligament will become sore and inflamed. This may take time to develop, so you may not feel pain at the time. Instead, you frequently have back ache the next day. If this is the case, change your exercise programme.

If a bent position of the spine is held regularly, perhaps as part of your job, overstretched ligaments will lengthen and those which are relaxed will shorten markedly. This is what happens with poor posture (*see* pages 27–39). If you are the sort of person who spends most of their day slumped in a chair, your spinal ligaments will alter, making it harder for you to hold your spine in a correct alignment when you stand up. To correct this, you must practise exercises to correct your spinal alignment and try to correct your general posture throughout the day.

> • • • • • • • • • • • • • • • **KEYPOINT** • • • • • • • • • • • • • • • •
> Repeated bending movements overstretch the spine and can damage it. Cut down on your bending!

NERVES •

The spinal cord consists of thousands of tiny nerve fibres bunched together much like a telephone cable. In the same way as the telephone line, the nerves carry electrical messages. When you want to move your leg, for example, an electrical message is sent from the brain. It travels down a nerve contained in your spinal cord to the muscles in your leg, commanding them to move.

A similar message can move in the opposite direction. If you touch a hot object, an electrical message is sent from your hand up a nerve in your arm through the spinal cord and to the area in your brain responsible for feeling. At any time, thousands of electrical impulses are travelling up and down the nerves in your body. If something blocks these impulses, the electrical messages change, and both movement and feeling can be affected. This is what happens when you trap a nerve. The nerve becomes compressed, a little like stepping on a hose pipe. When this happens the impulses for movement and feeling can become blocked, you get tingling sensations and numbness, and your muscles may twitch or become weak. These sensations can be felt wherever the nerve travels. Often with the lower back the feelings travel into the buttock and leg and then right down to the foot.

• • • • • • • • • • • • • • • • *KEYPOINT* • • • • • • • • • • • • • • • •
Pain or 'strange feelings' in your leg could be caused by an injury to your back.

DISC STRUCTURE, FUNCTION AND INJURY • • • • • • • • • •

The disc is the structure which separates the bodies of the two adjacent spinal bones. The disc acts like a shock absorber, preventing the spine from being shaken or jarred when we walk and run. Each disc has a hard outer casing which contains a softer spongy gel called the 'disc nucleus' (*see* fig. 5). Importantly, this gel has no direct blood supply, but instead relies on movement for its health. As the spine moves, fluids are pressed into the disc nucleus and waste products are squeezed out, keeping the disc healthy. As we get older the disc gel begins to dry up and becomes more brittle. When this happens the spine gets stiffer, and so you are no longer able to turn the cartwheels of your youth when you retire! However, through regular exercise, the disc stays springy for longer.

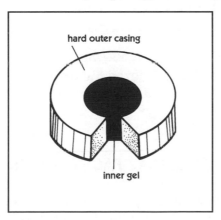

hard outer casing

inner gel

Fig.5 *The structure of the spinal disc*

If we were to look at the discs of someone who is 30 years old but inactive, and compare them to someone who is 40 but fit, the two discs would probably be exactly the same. The discs of the fitter person have stayed younger because they have been fed through regular movement.

```
• • • • • • • • • • • • • • • KEYPOINT • • • • • • • • • • • • • • • • •
          The disc needs regular movement to stay healthy.
```

As we move the spine, the spinal bones tip forwards and backwards, and as they do so they press the discs out of shape. When this happens the gel in the disc is squeezed and its pressure increases. Because we bend forwards much more often than we bend backwards, the gel in the disc starts to move backwards towards the delicate nerves of the spine. When this happens we begin to get pain. Initially this is a dull ache which occurs only occasionally. If we continue to do too much bending, however, we will begin to feel the pain more regularly and it will be more intense as the disc gradually becomes more damaged. Eventually, after many years of repeated bending, the gel in the centre of the disc can burst out and press on to one of the delicate nerves. When this happens it is termed a 'slipped disc', a particularly painful condition.

It is important to remember that it is *repeated* bending, stressing the disc over and over again, which is the real villain here. More people suffer from back pain brought on by bending the spine, through slumping in a poor chair or stooping when they work, than from lifting a heavy weight.

```
• • • • • • • • • • • • • • • KEYPOINT • • • • • • • • • • • • • • • • •
       Repeated bending squeezes the discs. Over many years
    damage accumulates and the discs can suddenly burst. This
                        is a slipped disc.
```

THE IMPORTANCE OF SPINAL FACET JOINTS • • • • • • • • •

The 'facets' are two small joints at the back of the vertebrae. They are similar in construction to other joints in the body in that they are contained within a tough leathery bag called a 'capsule'. As we bend forwards, the facet joint opens up, and as we bend back the joint closes. Twisting the spine results in the surfaces of the facet joint sliding over each other (*see* fig. 6).

Because these joints are so small, rapid movements can cause them to move too far and so damage them. Bending forwards repeatedly when practising stretching exercises, for example, can overstretch the leathery capsule of the facet joints, leaving the spine looser than it should be and therefore susceptible to injury. Bending backwards suddenly, as can be seen in some weight training exercises, closes the facet joints rapidly with a sudden 'jolt'. Over time this can cause premature wearing of these delicate joints.

Fig.6 *Spinal joint movement: (a) bending opens the spinal joints; (b) reaching up closes the spinal joints; (c) twisting causes the spinal joints to slide over each other*

•••••••••••••••• *KEYPOINT* ••••••••••••••••
Rapid movements can jolt the small facet joints at the back of
the spine, over and over again.

RANGE OF MOVEMENT ••••••••••••••••••••••••••••

The total extent of movement which is possible at any joint is
called its 'range of movement'. Normally, in everyday living we
operate with our joints moving in the middle of this range. This
is really the safest part because the joint is in no danger of being
overstretched and the muscles feel comfortable.

With each movement, damage can only occur if the joint is
pressed as far as it can go. We call this end point of movement
the 'end range'. When we are exercising, if we push our joints to
the end range over and over again we can damage them. A safer
method is to practise exercises for which the great majority of
movements are in the middle of the movement range. In this
way there is a good margin of safety (*see* fig. 7). In the F.L.A.T.
programme almost all of the exercises are performed using the
spine in the middle of its range of movement to guard against
injury.

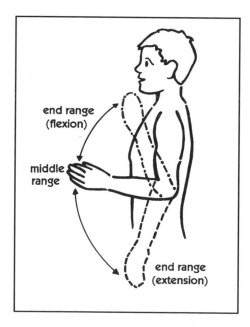

Fig.7 Range of movement

LUMBAR AND PELVIC MOVEMENTS • • • • • • • • • • • • • • •

Excessive movement in the lumbar spine can occur without us
noticing it. If a person bends forwards to touch their toes or
backwards to look at the ceiling, the movement is obvious. But
there is another way that the lumbar spine can move which is
more subtle.

The pelvis is connected directly to the lumbar spine (*see* fig. 8)
and in turn balances rather like a seesaw on the hip joints.
Because it is balanced, the pelvis can tilt forwards and backwards. As it tilts, the pelvis pulls the spine with it. If the pelvis
tips down (*see* fig. 8a) the arch in the lumbar spine increases in a
way equivalent to moving the spine backwards into 'extension'.
When the pelvis tilts up (*see* fig. 8c) the lumbar curve is flattened, and the movement in the lumbar spine is equivalent to
'flexion', or forward bending.

If the movement of the pelvis is excessive, the spine in turn is
pulled to its end range, stressing the spinal tissues. Note that
it is only the lumbar spine which is moving. The rest of the spine
remains largely unchanged, so the person is still standing
upright.

Fig.8 *Pelvic movement: (a) forward tilting – lower back hollow;*
(b) normal – lower back neutral; (c) backward tilting – lower back
flattens

> •••••••••••••••• *KEYPOINT* •••••••••••••••••
> Movement of the pelvis directly affects the lumbar spine.

THE NEUTRAL POSITION OF THE LUMBAR SPINE • • • • • • •

We have seen that as we move the spine the alignment of the spinal bones and tissues change. For example, as we flex forwards the facet joints open and the tissues on the back of the spine stretch while those on the front relax. At the same time the pressure within the spinal discs increases. This combination of pressure and stretch, if repeated over and over again, can damage the spinal tissues.

If, however, we align the spinal tissues so the spine is upright and the lumbar region is comfortably curved, the spinal tissues are now at their normal length and the pressure within the discs is lowered. We call this normal alignment of the spine the 'neutral position'. It is one of the safest postures for the spine, so all the elementary F.L.A.T. exercises begin with the spine in the neutral position.

To find your own neutral position, stand with your back to a wall. Your buttocks and shoulders should touch the wall. Place the flat of your hand between the wall and the small of your back. Try to tilt your pelvis so you flatten your back and then tilt your pelvis the other way so you increase the hollow in the lower back. Your neutral position (and it is slightly different for each person) is half way between the flat and hollow positions.

You should be able to just place the flat of your hand between your back and the wall. If you can only place your fingers through, your back is too flat; if your whole hand up to your wrist can pass through the space your back is too hollow.

> •••••••••••••••• *KEYPOINT* •••••••••••••••••
> In the neutral position the spine is correctly aligned and the spinal tissues are held at the right length.

SUMMARY

- The spine is divided into regions: cervical (neck), thoracic (rib cage), lumbar (lower back), sacrum and coccyx (tailbone).
- The spine forms an 'S' curve, making it naturally springy.
- Bending and straightening the spine stretches and relaxes the spinal ligaments.
- Nerves transmit electrical messages for movement and feeling.
- If a nerve is trapped, movement and feeling can alter, giving weakness, pain or tingling.
- The disc contains a gel and acts as a shock absorber.
- Safe movement keeps the discs healthy, but poor movements allow stress to build in the discs over many years.
- Mid-range is the centre part of the total extent of movement possible at a joint.
- In its neutral position, the spine is correctly aligned and the spinal tissues are at their normal length.

The trunk muscles

The abdominal muscles •

There are four principal abdominal muscles that concern us in the F.L.A.T. programme. In addition to these, we must be aware of the influence that the hip and back muscles have on the pelvis and lower spine, as this will affect our training.

In the centre of the abdomen is the 'rectus abdominis'. This muscle runs from the lower ribs to the pubic region, forming a narrow strap. It tapers down from about 6 in (15 cm) wide at the top to 3 in (8 cm) wide at the bottom. The muscle has three fibrous bands across it at the level of the tummy button, and above and below this point (*see* fig. 9a). The rectus muscle on each side of the body is contained within a sheath, the two sheaths merging in the centre line of the body via a strong fibrous band. This region splits during pregnancy to allow for the bulk of the developing child.

At the side of the abdomen there are two diagonal muscles, the 'internal oblique' (*see* fig. 9e) and the 'external oblique' (*see* fig. 9d). The internal oblique attaches to the front of the pelvic bone and a strong ligament in this region. From here it travels up and across to the lower ribs and into the sheath covering the rectus muscle. The external oblique has a similar position, but lies at an angle to the internal oblique. The external oblique begins from the lower eight ribs and travels to the sheath covering the rectus muscle and to the strong pelvic ligaments. The fibres in the centre of the muscle are travelling diagonally, but those right on the edge are travelling vertically and will assist the rectus muscle in its action.

Underneath the oblique abdominals lies the 'transversus muscle'. This attaches from the pelvic bones and tissue covering the spinal muscles and travels horizontally forwards to merge with the sheath covering the rectus muscle (*see* fig. 9c).

The muscles work together, and so in any action involving the abdomen, most of the muscles will be active to a certain extent. In a sit-up action, the upper portion of the rectus is emphasised, while in pelvic tilting the lower portion of this muscle and the outer fibres of the external oblique are used more. Twisting actions involve the oblique abdominals, while the transversus acting with the obliques pulls the tummy in tight. This muscle is used in coughing and sneezing as well.

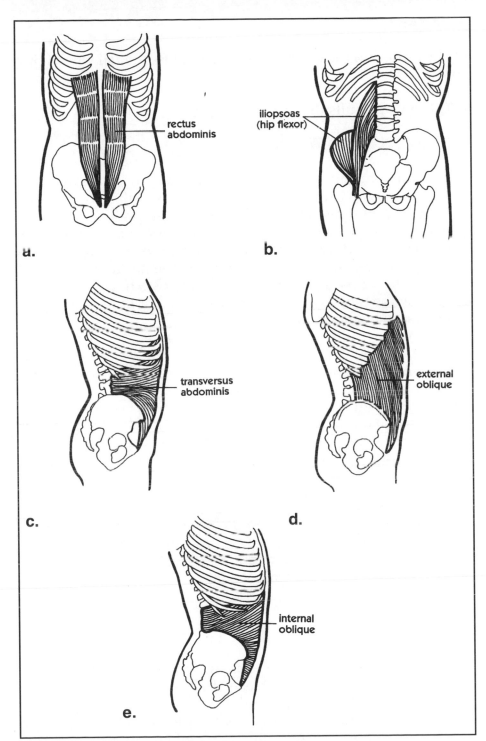

Fig.9 *The abdominal and hip flexor muscles*

SUMMARY

- The rectus muscle bends the trunk and lifts the tail when lying on the back.
- The obliques twist the spine.
- Transversus pulls the tummy in tight.

WHICH MUSCLES TO WORK

The abdominal muscles can either be used for movement, to bend or twist the trunk for example, or for stability. When used for stability, the muscles hold the spine firm, preventing excessive movement. In order to do this, they work to make the trunk into a more solid cylinder. For instance, when we are lifting something or pushing and pulling, the spine has to form a solid base for the arms and legs to push against. If not, the force created by the limbs will move the trunk rather than moving the object it was intended to.

Any of the trunk muscles can be activated by appropriate exercises to move the spine. However, to stabilise the spine it is the muscles deep inside the body, and therefore next to the spine, which are used. The transversus and the deep back muscles are your most important stability muscles, and they are helped by the obliques. The rectus muscle and the muscles near the surface of the back are responsible for rapid movements such as sitting up from lying, or standing up straight again from a bent over position.

> **•••••••••••••••• KEYPOINT ••••••••••••••••••**
> The deep trunk muscles make the spine more stable, holding the spinal bones together. The muscles on the surface cause movement.

THE HIP MUSCLES

The major hip muscle affected during abdominal training is the 'hip flexor' ('iliopsoas'). It attaches in two parts. The first part comes from the lumbar spine, the second from the pelvis (*see* fig. 9b). Both parts merge to fasten on to the thighbone. The action of this muscle is best illustrated when lying flat on your back. If you lift one leg, the hip flexor has acted to bend the hip.

If you sit up from lying flat, keeping your back straight and bending at the hip, the muscle has acted to pull your trunk up.

Because the muscle attaches to each vertebra of the lumbar spine, as it contracts it will pull the lumbar vertebrae together. As this happens the pressure within the vertebra will increase – we have seen that increased pressure within the disc is one cause of lower back pain. For this reason all the exercises used in the F.L.A.T. programme aim to reduce the work of the hip flexor. Where this muscle is working, the lumbar spine must be kept in its neutral position.

● ● ● ● ● ● ● ● ● ● ● ● ● ● ● ● *KEYPOINT* ● ● ● ● ● ● ● ● ● ● ● ● ● ● ● ●
If the hip flexor muscle is worked too hard it will pull on the lower spine, dangerously increasing the pressure within the discs.

HOW MUSCLES CAUSE MOVEMENT ● ● ● ● ● ● ● ● ● ● ● ● ● ●

Muscle consists of many fibres running parallel to each other. If we look through a microscope at these fibres we see that they contain a series of interlocking finger-like projections. When a muscle contracts, the finger projections pull together and overlap, shortening the muscle. So, as a muscle contracts it will pull. This is all it can do; it cannot push. For example, if you bend your arm the muscles on the inside of the arm pull the forearm towards the upper arm. The muscles on the outside of the arm cannot push the arm into this position. They must actually relax to allow the movement to occur.

The more the finger projections within the muscle can overlap, the stronger the muscle will be. If the muscle starts from a position where the projections are already overlapped and the muscle is shortened, the force the muscle can produce is very small because there is little further movement available. If the muscle is overstretched, the finger-like projections can't overlap sufficiently and so again the muscle appears weak. For maximum strength gains then, the muscle should be contracted from a comfortable lengthened position, not too short (cramped) or overstretched.

The other function of a muscle is to act like a giant elastic band. When stretched, the tissue within the muscle will spring back, and we call this 'recoil' or 'elastic strength'. When we look at the abdominal muscles during an exercise, we must consider how each muscle is acting to create a movement, and how it could limit a movement because of its length.

● ● ● ● ● ● ● ● ● ● ● ● ● ● ● ● ● *KEYPOINT* ● ● ● ● ● ● ● ● ● ● ● ● ● ● ● ●
A muscle can only pull; it cannot push.

ABDOMINAL MUSCLES AND PREGNANCY ● ● ● ● ● ● ● ● ● ●

During pregnancy the abdominal muscles have to stretch to accommodate the growing child. The muscles are able to stretch lengthways quite substantially, but their ability to stretch sideways is limited. The sideways increase in space is brought about by splitting of the tissue which joins the two neighbouring rectus muscles in the centre line of the body (*see* fig. 10). The split is called a 'diastasis' and its size is dependent on a number of factors. Mothers who have a narrow pelvis or a large baby (over 9 lbs) are likely to have a large diastasis, as are those who have twins or triplets. If a mother has been inactive during her pregnancy or has not toned up the abdominal muscles following a previous pregnancy, again the diastasis may be larger.

During pregnancy the abdominal hollowing action and pelvic tilting (*see* pages 72–81) are important to reduce the strain on the abdominal wall and the spine. Following child birth, the diastasis must be allowed to close before very active abdominal exercises are begun. Abdominal hollowing is particularly useful

Fig.10 *The abdominal muscles in pregnancy: (a) normal; (b) following child birth*

during the early stages (from three days following child birth). The action should be practised regularly throughout the day to re-educate the abdominal muscles. It is often easier to practise this movement while breast feeding in a sitting or lying position: the young mother has little time available, and the feeding period may be the only respite she has.

Pelvic tilting is also important during the first weeks after child birth. The aim now is to correct any exaggerated 'lordosis' which occurs through a forward tilted pelvis (*see* fig. 8a, page 9). Whenever the young mum is standing, she should try to do so without an excessive curve in the lower spine.

The oblique abdominal muscles pull on to the area of the tummy which has split during pregnancy. Forcible contraction of the obliques may therefore slow the closure of the diastasis, so twisting actions against resistance should not be practised until the diastasis has closed to a width of two fingers.

SUMMARY

• The split in the abdominal muscles which occurs during pregnancy is called a 'diastasis'.
• The diastasis may be larger if you have a narrow pelvis, or if you have a large baby or twins.
• The diastasis may be larger if you are overweight or have poor abdominal tone.
• The abdominal hollowing exercise can help regain your figure.
• Vigorous abdominal training is dangerous after pregnancy.
• Correct posture is important after pregnancy to help prevent back pain.

BASIC CONCEPTS OF ABDOMINAL TRAINING

EFFECTIVE MUSCLE STRENGTHENING ● ● ● ● ● ● ● ● ● ● ● ●

For a muscle to become stronger, it must be worked harder than it would be in everyday activities. When it is, we say that the muscle has been 'overloaded'. To achieve this degree of muscle work, we must decide on the type of exercise required, and its duration, frequency of use and intensity.

The type of exercise will dictate the type of strength we will build up. There are three major sorts of strength, termed 'isometric', 'concentric' and 'eccentric'. Isometric strength occurs when we tense a muscle and hold it tight. It is the type of strength needed to hold a joint still and to stop it moving. Concentric strength occurs when a muscle is shortening and speeding up a movement. It is the type used when we pick something up, for example. Eccentric strength is exactly the reverse. During eccentric activity the muscle begins to shorten and is gradually 'let out'. It is the type of activity used when lowering a weight in a controlled fashion.

The three types of muscle work can be illustrated when standing up and sitting down in a chair. As we stand up the thigh muscles are tightening and working concentrically. If we stop ourselves just short of full standing and hold the position, the same muscles work isometrically. As we slowly lower ourselves down again back into the chair, the muscles are working eccentrically. All three types of muscle work are important to the abdominals, and so all three are used in the F.L.A.T. programme.

● ● ● ● ● ● ● ● ● ● ● ● ● ● *KEYPOINT* ● ● ● ● ● ● ● ● ● ● ● ● ●
The three types of muscle action are concentric (lifting),
isometric (holding), and eccentric (lowering).

The intensity (how hard), duration (how long) and frequency (how often) of exercises used in the F.L.A.T. programme are also important. Too little exercise will fail to achieve the results we want. Too much will lead to overtraining, leaving us stale and possibly leading ultimately to injury. The intensity and duration of exercise are dictated by the type of muscles we are using. The abdominal muscles work mainly to tense and hold the trunk steady during everyday activities. To do this, the muscles will require endurance, so that they can continue to work for long periods. This may be achieved by working the muscles at slightly less than half of their maximum strength. When the muscles contract, we try to build up the length of time they can hold the contraction until eventually we can hold the abdominal muscles tight for 30 seconds or so.

Where the abdominal muscles are used in sport, in addition to their role of supporting the trunk by holding it tight, they may be used in dynamic actions to rapidly move the trunk. In this case, the muscles must be trained for power and speed. It is important to note that the supporting (stabilising) function of the abdominal muscles is always re-trained first in the F.L.A.T. programme. Only when this has been achieved, and an athlete has good control of trunk alignment and movement, should power movements begin. The restoration of good support in the trunk forms the foundation upon which other types of training may be built.

The frequency of practice will change as we progress through the programme. This is because initially the intention is to learn correct exercise technique. When learning technique, we aim for a high number of short practice bouts to help concentration. For the F.L.A.T. programme most exercises are practised twice daily to begin with. The only exception is abdominal hollowing which is practised regularly throughout the day during everyday activities. Once the techniques of the exercises have been mastered, the number of practice bouts reduces and the exercises become harder. Harder exercise will require a longer recovery period, and so exercises are now practised every other day, leaving a full day inbetween to allow the muscles to recover.

•••••••••••••••• *KEYPOINT* ••••••••••••••••
When deciding on an exercise, consider its type (which muscles are working), duration (how long it lasts), frequency (how often it is performed), and intensity (how hard it is).

THE PRINCIPLE OF TRAINING SPECIFICITY • • • • • • • • • •

When a muscle is strengthened, its make-up actually changes. The muscle becomes larger and tighter, and there are alterations in the chemicals it contains. In addition, the way the brain controls the movement itself becomes smoother and more co-ordinated. All of these changes constitute what we call the 'training adaptation'. In other words the changes which the body makes are a direct result of the training itself. The exact adaptation will closely reflect the type of exercise which has been used, and so we say that the muscle adaptation is 'specific' to the demands placed upon it.

An example from general sport may make this clearer. Imagine two people who run marathons. They want to reduce their times and go for a 'personal best'. If one person trains by running long distances and the other by running short sprints, who will be more successful in reducing their times? The answer is the person who runs distances. This type of training more accurately reflects the actions required during marathon running. Marathon runners need endurance. Short sprints will build mainly strength and speed, and so although the person using sprint training is getting fitter, the fitness is not the type required for the final marathon race. His body has changed (adapted) but these changes do not closely match those needed for running the marathon, they are not truly 'specific'.

> • • • • • • • • • • • • • • • • **KEYPOINT** • • • • • • • • • • • • • • • • •
> For an exercise to be truly 'specific' it must closely match the action which we hope to improve.

When training the trunk muscles the same principles of specificity apply. We need to know what function the trunk muscles perform, and then tailor our training programme to improve this function. We have already seen that trunk muscle function falls broadly into two categories, support or stabilisation, and movement. During stabilisation the trunk muscles work mainly isometrically (tense and hold) to make the trunk more solid. During movement the muscles work concentrically and eccentrically to perform actions such as bending and twisting. Importantly however, the trunk must be stable before more rapid movements can be attempted, and our training should take this into account.

> •••••••••••••••• **KEYPOINT** ••••••••••••••••••
> The trunk muscles must be able to effectively hold the spine in
> a stable position before any vigorous trunk exercise is
> attempted.

During the F.L.A.T. programme we are aiming initially to restore the ability of the trunk muscles to stabilise the spine. Only when this has been achieved do we work on the muscles' ability to move the spine and provide power. For this reason, the initial part of the programme works the muscles responsible for stability and re-trains their ability to tense and hold the trunk still. At this stage, if rapid movements such as sit-ups are used, they could damage the spine. Rapid actions are not specific to stabilisation and until you are able to stabilise your spine and control it, rapid actions are dangerous.

Later, when stability has been re-trained, movements may begin. Initially they are slow and controlled and later they build up speed and power. At this later stage, the movements practised mimic the actions used in sport. In this way the training remains specific to a subject's individual sport.

> •••••••••••••••• **KEYPOINT** ••••••••••••••••••
> The F.L.A.T. programme begins by improving spinal stability
> and moves on to improve general movements.

FITNESS COMPONENTS ••••••••••••••••••••••••••••••

Physical fitness may be defined as a person's ability to perform a physical task. Fitness may be seen on a continuum from an optimal level seen in the competitive athlete, through to the minimal standard required to stay healthy, and finally to a complete lack of fitness and the development of ill health (*see* fig. 11a). Fitness, then, is not simply a lack of disease, it is more than this. It is the ability of the body to allow a person to live a happy and well balanced life.

We can think of fitness in two parts. There is health-related fitness which involves items directly related to improving health and preventing disease. But also, there is task- or performance-related fitness which involves factors necessary for a person to perform a particular sport, or an activity at work for example. To make things easier we can divide fitness into a series of components or 'S' factors (*see* fig. 11b).

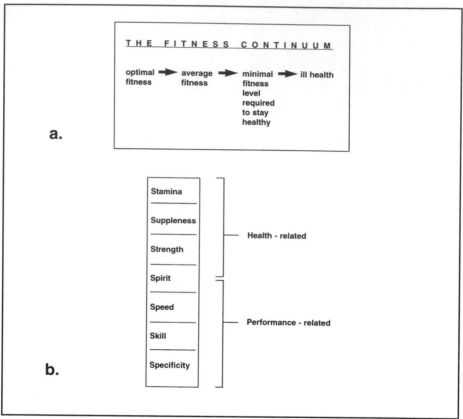

Fig.11 Physical fitness

• **Stamina** encompasses heart-lung fitness and also muscle endurance, or the ability to keep an exercise going.
• **Suppleness** (flexibility) and **Strength** are both essential to the health of the joints.
• **Spirit** involves psychological factors which are important to both health and sport, such as motivation, how satisfied a person is with their own body, and a positive outlook on life.
• **Speed** (also encompassing power) is needed for explosive actions in sport.
• **Skill** is important to all actions, but especially those involving complex movements.
• **Specificity**, as we have seen, is important when matching exercise to sports actions.

The important point about the components of fitness is that they must be balanced. Often, exercise works on one component but not on others. For example, intensive bodybuilding may provide dramatic gains in strength, but little improvement in suppleness or stamina. Running marathons will generate a high degree of stamina, but little suppleness or strength in the upper body.

When the fitness components become imbalanced, the body may be pulled out of alignment and injury can result. For example, if muscles are strong but not supple they will tend to pull or 'strain' more easily. If a joint is too supple it will have little stability and may give way. The aim with fitness is to improve all components more or less equally.

> • • • • • • • • • • • • • • • **KEYPOINT** • • • • • • • • • • • • • • • • •
> All the fitness components must be balanced for optimal health.

Skill is often a fitness component which is forgotten. In the race to lift heavier weights, to stretch further or run faster, the quality of an exercise frequently takes a back seat to quantity. But as with so many things in life, more is not necessarily better. If the quality of a movement suffers, injury is more likely because an action becomes clumsy. In the F.L.A.T. programme we are aiming for *quality* of movement before quantity with every single exercise. The initial movements aim to re-educate the basic skills of spinal movement which have often lain dormant since childhood. This is essential because it forms the foundation for the whole programme. A person must be able to perform an exercise in a smooth, controlled fashion before the number of repetitions is increased.

> • • • • • • • • • • • • • • • **KEYPOINT** • • • • • • • • • • • • • • • • •
> The quality (control) of an exercise is more important than the quantity (number of repetitions) that can be performed.

CONTROLLING THE NEUTRAL SPINAL POSITION • • • • • • • •

One of the most basic movements that you will need to control is pelvic tilting. You must be able to recognise when the pelvis tilts and pulls the spine out of alignment during everyday activities. Ideal alignment of the spine is a position where the pelvis is mid-way between being tilted fully back and fully forwards. We call this the 'neutral position' of the spine. In the neutral position, the joints, discs, and tissues are subjected to loads which they were designed to withstand. When we move away from the neutral position, stress on some tissues reduces but stress on others increases dramatically. The neutral position is therefore a 'safety zone' for the spine.

The practical methods used to find the neutral position were detailed earlier. Once you have mastered the neutral position, use it regularly throughout the day and during all exercises. Try to sit in a chair with your spine in its neutral position. If you are in a gym using weight training apparatus, perform the exercise with your spine in its neutral position. When you are using stretching exercises, again try to keep the spine in its neutral position for as long as possible.

> • • • • • • • • • • • • • • • **KEYPOINT** • • • • • • • • • • • • • • • • •
> The spine is in its neutral position when the pelvis is level and the lower back is slightly hollow. Use the neutral position as often as possible to safeguard your back.

PROGRESSIVE EXERCISE •

We have seen that to train the body we must overload it; that is, make the body work harder than it would normally during everyday activities. However, as fitness improves, the same amount of activity becomes easier and no longer taxes the body to the same degree. The training effect therefore reduces. To maintain the overload and continue to work the body sufficiently, the exercise must get harder as we become fitter. We now say that the exercise is 'progressing'.

> • • • • • • • • • • • • • • • **KEYPOINT** • • • • • • • • • • • • • • • • •
> Over time, as an exercise becomes easier we must progress it (make it harder) to maintain the training effect.

One of the ways of progressing a weight training exercise is to perform a greater number of lifts (repetitions) with each training session. To progress stamina when running, we could simply run a longer distance with each training session. But there are other methods of progressing an exercise without increasing the amount of training that we do.

One such method of progressing an exercise is to increase the degree of leverage the body is subjected to. In a sit-up action, for example, if the arms are held by the sides the weight of the upper body acts in the centre of the trunk, and the distance between the pivot point of the action (the hip joint) and the weight of the body represents a lever. If the arms are placed behind the head, their weight has moved away from the pivot point and so the leverage effect is greater. If the arms are held above the head, again the leverage has increased so the exercise has progressed (*see* fig. 12). In each case the weight of the body has obviously remained the same, but the increasing leverage effect has placed an additional overload on the working muscles.

Fig.12 *Progressing an exercise using leverage. As the arms move higher up the body, the leverage distance between the hip and arm weight increases.*

A second method of exercise progression is to change the type of work a muscle has to perform. When a muscle is working against a load, for example when trying to lift a weight, it can work in three ways. If the muscle can create enough force to move the load it is working concentrically. If it can only create enough force to hold the load still it is working isometrically. If it can't lift the weight or even hold it, but can make the weight lower more slowly, it is working eccentrically. An eccentric action is therefore easier than an isometric action and this in turn is easier than a concentric action. If a muscle is very weak we should therefore begin with eccentric or isometric work (lowering or holding) before we move on to concentric work (lifting).

Adding resistance is another method of exercise progression for strength. The resistance may be anything which makes the movement harder. Elastic bands, springs, weights, and even the resistance of moving through water, will all strengthen muscle more effectively than free movement.

POSTURE

Posture is simply the relationship or 'alignment' between the various parts of the body. It is important from two standpoints. Firstly, good posture underlies all exercise techniques. Your posture is really your foundation for movement. In the same way that a building will fall down if its foundations are shaky, your whole body will suffer if your posture is poor. Exercises which begin from the basis of poor posture tend to be awkward and clumsy. Because of this they are less effective, and more importantly, the person using awkward, clumsy movements is likely to be injured.

The second important point about posture is that an incorrect posture allows physical stress to build up in certain tissues, ultimately leading to pain and injury. For example, a person who is very round-shouldered may simply have started out with tightness in the chest muscles and weakness in the muscles which brace the shoulders back. If this combination had been corrected at the time, the poor posture may not have built up over the years. As a consequence of poor posture, the way that the joints move will change. Alteration in movement of this type will mean that joints can be subjected to uneven stresses. When this continues over the years, the eventual outcome can be the development of 'osteoarthritis' in later life.

We saw earlier that fitness is really a combination of various components which we called 'S' factors. In relation to posture the two most important fitness components are flexibility and strength. Postural changes are often associated with poor muscle tone (weakness) in some muscles together with too much tone (tightening) in others. This imbalance in tone gives an uneven pull from the muscles around a joint, and causes the joint to move off-centre (*see* fig. 13). Our aim with exercise is to redress the balance in muscle tone by using stretching exercises to lengthen tight muscles, combined with strengthening exercises to increase the tone of lax muscles.

• • • • • • • • • • • • • • • **KEYPOINT** • • • • • • • • • • • • • • • •
Your posture will affect the way you exercise, and the
exercises you choose will in turn alter your posture.

Fig.13 *Posture and muscle imbalance: (a) normal joint – equal muscle tone gives correct joint alignment; (b) postural imbalance – unequal muscle tone pulls joint out of alignment.*

OPTIMAL POSTURE ●

We cannot talk about a normal posture because very few people are 'normal' in the true sense of the word. Equally, if we talk about an average posture, the average may be very poor and this type of posture is far from ideal. Instead we should talk about an 'optimal' posture, where the various body segments are aligned correctly, and the minimum of stress is placed on the body tissues. This type of posture requires little muscle activity to maintain it because it is essentially balanced.

The various segments of the body work together like the links in a chain. Movement in one causes movement in the next link which is then passed on to the next, and so on. This means that a postural change in one part of the body can alter the alignment of another bodypart quite far away. Alterations in the feet are a good illustration of this point. Flat feet, where the inner arch of the foot moves downwards, will in turn twist the shinbone and then the thighbone. Eventually these changes can be felt in the lower back, chest and neck. Because of this intimate link between body segments, it is important to correct any postural fault, however minor it may seem at the time.

One method of looking at posture is to compare it to the posture line. In an optimal posture this line is similar to a plumb line dropped vertically downwards from the top of the head. The body should be evenly distributed along this line (*see* fig. 14), and ideally the line should pass just in front of the knee, travel through the hip and shoulder joints and through the ear. Looking more closely at the pelvis, optimal pelvic alignment occurs when the lip of the pelvis is in a direct vertical line with the pubic bone in the groin. In this position there should be a gentle curve to the lumbar spine and a gentle curve to the neck. However, various alterations occur from this normal posture line with which we need to concern ourselves.

through ear

through shoulder joint

through hip joint

in front of ankle

the posture line

Fig.14 *The optimal posture: the lip of the pelvis forms a near vertical line with the pubic bone in the groin.*

ASSESSING YOUR OWN POSTURE • • • • • • • • • • • • • •

Before we can correct posture using the F.L.A.T. exercises, we must make an assessment to determine your current body alignment. You will need to work with a partner; they will assess your posture and you in turn will assess theirs. Ask your partner to stand against a straight vertical edge, such as a doorframe, or plumb line attached to a hook. Make sure that the edge of the line is slightly in front of their anklebone and then compare their posture to this reference line. Fig. 14 shows the posture line, together with the optimal alignment. Photocopy this diagram, and then mark on the sheet the positions of their knee, hip, shoulder and ear. It is the centre point of each of these that we are interested in. The next step is to determine the position of your partner's pelvis. Draw an imaginary line from the rim of the pelvis (the furthest point forwards) to their pubic bone. Determine whether this line is vertical or positioned at an angle.

Once you have assessed your partner's posture from the side, turn them around so that their back is towards you. Their feet should be about 4 in (10 cm) apart. We will now continue the postural assessment using fig. 15. Start by looking at the feet. The inner edge of the foot should have a gentle arch, and should not be flat. Moving up the leg, the Achilles tendon should be vertical and the bulk of the calf muscles should be equal. The creases on the back of the knees and the lower edge of the buttocks should be on the same level for both sides of the body. The pelvis itself should be level horizontally and the spine aligned vertically. One of the ways that spinal alignment can be checked is to look at the skin creases on either side of the lower trunk; they should be equal in number and shape. The shoulder blades should be about three finger breadths apart, and they should lie on the same horizontal line. The contours of the shoulders should be on the same level and they should appear similar in size and shape. Finally, the head should be level and not tilted to one side. Record any changes from the optimal posture on a photocopy of fig. 15.

The final method of posture assessment is to establish the depth of the curve in the lower back. Ideally, the curve should be gently hollow. When it is too deep, or too flat, the alignment of the lumbar region changes, indicating that the pelvic tilt is no longer correct. We assess the depth of the lumbar curve by standing with the back up against a wall. Stand with the feet 6–8 in (15–20 cm) from the wall and the buttocks and shoulders

	POSITION OF BODYPART	YOUR SCORE
	Head position	
	Shoulder level	
	Position of shoulder blade contour	
	Skin creases at waist and spinal alignment	
	Level of buttock creases	
	Level of knee creases	
	Calf muscle bulk and Achilles alignment	
	Flat foot or high arch	

Fig.15 *Assessing standing posture from behind*

touching the wall (*see* fig. 16). Have your partner slide their hand between the wall and the small of your back. Ideally they should be able to push the hand through the gap only as far as the fingers (*see* fig. 16a). If the whole hand passes through (*see* fig. 16b) your lumbar curve is too deep. If they can only get the tips of the fingers between your back and the wall, the lumbar curve is too flat (*see* fig. 16c).

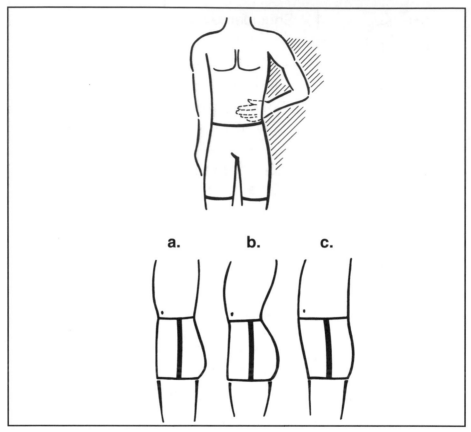

Fig.16 *Assessing the lumbar curve: (a) normal; (b) too deep; (c) too flat*

SUMMARY

In an optimal posture:
- the hip, shoulder and ear lie in a vertical line
- the pelvis is level
- the lower spine should be gently hollowed
- the inner edge of the shoulder blades are 4–5 in (10–12 cm) apart.

HOLLOW BACK POSTURE ●

In an optimal posture the pelvis should be level, with the front rim of the pelvis and the pubic bone in a vertical line when viewed from the side. In this position the lower part of the back (the lumbar spine) should be slightly hollowed. In the hollow back posture, however, the abdominal muscles become weak and lengthened, allowing the pelvis to tip forwards. When this happens the pull on the lumbar spine increases the lumbar curve. This increased curvature places stress on the discs and small joints (facet joints) of the lower spine. Over time, back pain can result. This can be particularly bad if a person stands for long periods.

The problem here is not abdominal strength but the length of the abdominal muscles, and the fact that the lower spine has been held in its hollow position for a long time. To correct the hollow back posture we must choose exercises which aim to shorten the abdominals. The abdominal hollowing exercise and trunk curl are the two which we use in the programme, and are described on pages 75 and 80 respectively. This type of posture is particularly common after pregnancy and is also seen in young female gymnasts, who choose this posture to walk.

The hollow back posture (*see* fig. 17a) is the classic 'beer belly' posture where many years of inactivity, combined with excess weight, leave the abdominals poorly toned. Often the angulation of the pelvis can shorten the hip flexor muscles and these will require stretching. The exercise we choose for this is shown in fig. 17b. Initially the person takes up a half-kneeling position and they perform the abdominal hollowing exercise to tighten and stabilise their trunk. From this position they then press themselves forwards, forcing their lower leg into extension, effectively stretching the hip flexors. It is essential when this exercise is performed that the lower spine does not hollow. When this happens the movement is occurring at the lumbar spine rather than the hip.

Where the posture has been present for many years, the base of the spine may be very stiff. Fig. 17c shows an exercise to relieve this stiffness. Lie flat on the floor with your knees bent. Grip your legs behind your knees and pull the knees up towards the chest. This will have the effect of rounding the lower spine in the opposite direction to the hollow back. Make sure that the movement is slow and controlled. Never force the spine to move if it is stiff, encourage it.

Fig.17 *Hollow back posture: (a) abdominal muscles sag; (b) hip flexor stretch; (c) knee-to-chest back stretch*

•••••••••••••••• ***KEYPOINT*** ••••••••••••••••
In the hollow back posture, the lumbar curve is excessive and the abdominal muscles are lengthened.

HEAD, NECK AND SHOULDER POSTURE

Head and neck posture are important considerations when using abdominal exercises. Often standard sit-up movements, placing the hands behind the neck, can lead to the development of poor posture in this region and subsequent pain.

When we look at a person from the side their shoulder joint and ear should be positioned on the posture line. A common postural abnormality associated with the upper spine is called the round back posture (*see* fig. 18a). Changes occur in the position of the head and neck, the shoulder joint and upper spine (thoracic spine). The normal curve of the thoracic region is lost and pain often develops between the shoulder blades.

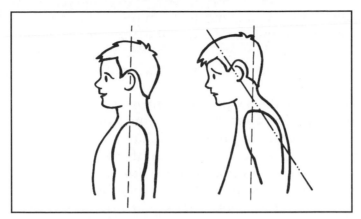

Fig.18(a) *Round back posture: normal (left); incorrect head and shoulder alignment (right)*

When we look at a person from the side, if they have the round back posture the head is often held forwards with the shoulders being excessively rounded. The chest muscles ('pectorals') are normally too tight, while the muscles that pull the shoulders back ('retractors') are often too weak. Looking at the person from the back, the shoulder blades should be roughly 3 in (8 cm) apart. However, in the round back posture, weakness of the shoulder muscles allows the shoulder blades to drop apart and to twist.

Our aim with this posture is to stretch the tight chest muscles, strengthen the weak shoulder muscles, and to stretch the muscles at the back of the neck. The first exercise we use to achieve this is shown in fig. 18b. A person lies flat on the floor

Fig.18(b) *Stretch*

35

with their arms spread into a 'T' shape. From this position the elbows are bent and the arms take up a 90° position. Simply holding this position will stretch the chest muscles and the muscles which twist the shoulders. Breathe slowly and try to relax into the movement.

To strengthen the upper back muscles a similar position is taken up, but this time lying on the front. Again the person stretches their arms out into a 'T' shape but this time they stay straight. The aim now is simply to lift the straight arms up by 2 in (5 cm) and to hold that position for 10 seconds (*see* fig. 18c). This will bring the shoulder blades together and strengthen the muscles surrounding these areas. Perform this movement five times, each time holding the position for 10 seconds.

Fig.18(c) *Strengthen*

Fig.18(d) *Draw head backwards, tuck chin in*

To stretch the neck muscles we perform a chin tuck movement. Stand upright with the head level. From this position, simply draw the chin inwards without looking up or down (*see* fig. 18d). This allows the neck to move on a single line, allowing the joints in the neck to glide freely. As you pull the chin in, the curve at the base of the neck is flattened and you should feel the muscles behind the neck stretching.

● ● ● ● ● ● ● ● ● ● ● ● ● ● ● ● ● ● *KEYPOINT* ● ● ● ● ● ● ● ● ● ● ● ● ● ● ● ● ●
In the round back posture the chin pokes forwards, and the shoulders are rounded. The chest muscles are tight, and the muscles controlling the shoulder blades are weak.

SWAYBACK POSTURE ●

We have seen that to assess posture we compare a person's body alignment to a vertical plumb line. In the swayback posture, the pelvis stays level but the hips move forwards of the posture line (*see* fig. 19). Because the hip joint now lies in front of the posture line, the hip is effectively pulled back into extension. In this position the hip flexor muscles are lengthened, exactly the opposite situation to that which we saw in the hollow back posture earlier. If we compare the normal and swayback postures, we can see that in a normal posture the furthest point forwards is the chest, while the furthest point backwards are the buttocks. In the swayback, however, the furthest point forwards is the abdomen, and the thoracic spine is the furthest point back.

Looking at the lower back in the normal posture, the lumbar curve is gently hollow along its whole length. In the swayback, however, the hollow is sharp and more pronounced in the lower region of the spine. Finally, in the normal posture the spine and leg are close to the posture line, but in the swayback the spine and leg form a curve with the person's whole body profile taking on the shape of a letter 'V' turned on its side. The swayback is a relaxed or slumped posture frequently seen in adolescents.

Correction of the swayback posture is accomplished through continuous practice of correct alignment rather than strength or stretching exercises. Because the bodyline in the swayback is curved, a person with this posture appears shorter. Simply by trying to stand tall, the swayback should correct itself.

Fig.19 *Swayback posture*

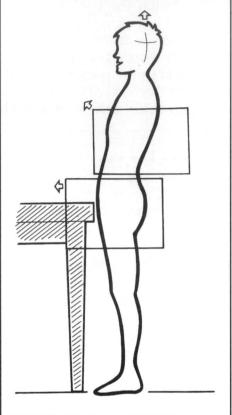

Fig.20 *Correction of swayback posture. Stand in front of a table. The chest moves forward and the spine is lengthened. Stand 'tall'*

Further improvement is achieved by practising correct body segment alignment with particular reference to the pelvis. Stand in front of a table with the edge of the table just touching the pelvis. Imagine your pelvis and chest to be two separate blocks (*see* fig. 20). Without bending, slide your chest forwards, trying to avoid pressing your pelvis harder into the table.

• • • • • • • • • • • • • • • • • **KEYPOINT** • • • • • • • • • • • • • • • •
In the swayback posture the hip and pelvis are thrust forwards, and the body slouches.

FLATBACK POSTURE ●

In the flatback posture, a person shows a markedly reduced lumbar curve. When standing straight with the spine up against a wall, you should normally be able to place the flat of your hand between the wall and your lower spine (see fig. 16, page 32). Someone with a flatback posture may only be able to place one or two fingers in the gap formed. In this posture, the pelvis has tilted backwards and the lumbar spine has been pulled with it. The flat-back is commonly seen where a person has spent a lot of time sitting slumped in a chair. It is particularly common after a bout of back pain where a person has rested in bed for too long. Stiffness may occur either when bending forwards or bending backwards, with the spine becoming almost fixed in the flatback position.

Stretching can help to alleviate the pain from this condition, providing it is performed gently to encourage movement rather than to force it. The stretching should feel slightly uncomfortable because the exercises are working on very tight structures. However, they should not give back pain, and in cases where this occurs exercise should only be carried out under the supervision of a physiotherapist. Start the stretch by lying flat on your front. Place your forearms down on the floor at the side of your chest. Keeping your hips down, push with your arms and arch the spine until you come up on your forearms (*see* fig. 21). Practise the exercise each day, and gradually the movement will come back.

Fig.21 *Correction of flatback posture*

● ● ● ● ● ● ● ● ● ● ● ● ● ● ● ● ● *KEYPOINT* ● ● ● ● ● ● ● ● ● ● ● ● ● ● ● ● ●
In the flatback posture the normal lumbar curve is lost, and the lower back appears stiff.

DIET AND EXERCISE

People often begin using abdominal exercises in the hope of reducing their waistline. They may join a local gym or exercise class and work hard for many months. Eventually, however, they can lose enthusiasm if they fail to see the results they wanted. Instead of reducing their waistline all they have achieved is a marginal re-shaping, and they give up exercising, disillusioned. There are two reasons for the failure of this type of training. Firstly, if exercise is not coupled with a correct diet, you will not lose significant amounts of weight. Secondly, the type of training will determine the effect it has on your waistline. The wrong type of training will often have little effect at all.

BODYWEIGHT AND BODYFAT ● ● ● ● ● ● ● ● ● ● ● ● ● ● ● ● ● ●

People often talk about being overweight, meaning that they have too much loose flesh around the abdomen (men), and around the abdomen, thighs and buttocks (women). However, your bodyweight is made up of a number of things. Bone, muscle, fluids, body organs, fat and other tissues all contribute to your total weight. Take a sauna and you will lose weight because you sweat out water, but this is not a permanent weight loss. Begin a weight training programme and your muscles will become sleek, firm and toned. This may be desirable, but because muscle weighs more than fat you may actually gain a few pounds. What we really mean when we say someone is overweight is that they have too much fat, possibly linked to flabby muscle.

Bodyfat occurs in different types. Essential bodyfat is found around the body organs and within the marrow in the centre of the bones. Women have more fat than men because they carry additional sex specific fat which is important for a variety of hormonal functions. If the level of fat is reduced too much, as can be the case in young girls who diet excessively, for example, a woman's periods will often stop due to the hormonal changes caused by the low bodyfat. The other type of fat is storage fat which is found beneath the skin and acts as a depot for energy. It is the storage fat which often becomes excessive.

In order to lose inches from the waistline we need to reduce the amount of bodyfat, while maintaining a healthy, balanced diet. But this must be coupled with exercise to tone and shape the muscles of the abdomen or they will remain flabby.

> • • • • • • • • • • • • • • • • **KEYPOINT** • • • • • • • • • • • • • • • • •
> The amount of bodyfat you have is more important than your weight.

THE FEEDING CONTROL MECHANISM ● ● ● ● ● ● ● ● ● ● ● ● ● ● ●

One of the main factors which assists in the control of an ideal bodyweight is the 'feeding control mechanism' (F.C.M.). This is situated within the brain in an area called the 'hypothalamus'. The F.C.M. controls bodyweight by matching the amount of energy obtained from food to the requirements of the body through activity. If the amount of energy going into the body is exactly equal to the amount going out, the bodyweight will remain constant. Individuals who are overweight tend to have lost the ability to precisely match their energy requirements to their diet. Unless the F.C.M. is re-set, long-term control of an ideal bodyweight is unlikely. One of the problems with crash diets is that although they lead to a short-term reduction in weight, because they restrict the amount of energy going in, the F.C.M. tries to conserve energy and the 'tick-over speed' of the body (the 'basal metabolic rate') is slowed by as much as 45%. This means that weight loss will slow down and a person can quickly lose motivation because they always desire more food than they are getting. When they stop the diet the weight goes back on again and we get a yo-yo effect of repeated weight loss and weight gain over a period of time.

A more effective method of weight control is to combine good dietary habits with regular activity, as this type of programme has been shown to re-set the F.C.M. to the correct levels.

> • • • • • • • • • • • • • • • • **KEYPOINT** • • • • • • • • • • • • • • • •
> The most effective way to trim yourself down, and keep that way, is to combine a high quality, balanced diet with regular exercise.

41

A NOTE ON CALORIES •

The energy taken into the body as food, and that expended during activity, is measured in calories, a measure of the heat a food would produce if it were burnt. One kilocalorie or Calorie (with a capital 'C') is the more common measure, and this is equivalent to 4.2 joules, the joule being the other measure of food energy sometimes seen on food packaging. Some of the main constituents of food are carbohydrate, which is a starchy or sugary material giving energy, fat, which is an energy store, and protein, used to build the body tissues. All of these substances can be used by the body for energy, and so may be measured in Calories. Both carbohydrate and protein produce the same amount of energy. Fat is a more concentrated energy source, and can produce more than double the energy of the other two foods. This is why fat is used as an energy store, and reducing it from the diet is a good way to lose weight. Another, and often overlooked, source of energy is alcohol which has almost the same number of Calories as fat.

Foods are made up of a mixture of nutrients, and so we give each food a total Calorie value, reflecting the proportional amounts of the various nutrients it contains. The Calorie value is useful when the food is used as part of a Calorie-controlled diet to lose weight, but does not relate to the quality of the food. This is because high-Calorie foods are not necessarily high in vitamins and minerals, and fibre contains virtually no Calories at all, but is still an important part of the diet.

Energy is used up by the body in two ways. Even without movement, the body has a certain 'resting energy' required for breathing, heartbeat, digestion and other important bodily functions. The amount of energy needed for these processes can vary from person to person depending on many factors, including body size. This resting energy is the basal metabolic rate, and normally uses up about 1200 Calories each day. The other requirement for energy comes from 'voluntary activity', including things such as manual work and exercise. People who have very active jobs, and those who exercise intensely, will burn up more Calories.

Different sports will burn off Calories at different rates. For example, slow jogging may use 120 Calories an hour, while driving a car needs only 48 Calories. Intense swimming or circuit weight training, where all the muscles are worked, can use over 250 Calories in the same time. In order to significantly burn Calories, the exercise should be continuous for 20–30 minutes and must be practised regularly.

LOSING WEIGHT ●

When the amount of energy (measured in Calories) taken into the body from food equals the amount being expended during exercise and everyday activities, we can say that a person is in 'energy balance'. In this situation he will neither gain nor lose weight. If the energy input is greater than the expenditure, the extra energy will be stored as fat. If too little energy is taken in, the body makes up the deficit by drawing on stored energy and burning up fat.

> ● ● ● ● ● ● ● ● ● ● ● ● ● ● ● *KEYPOINT* ● ● ● ● ● ● ● ● ● ● ● ● ● ● ●
> When the amount of energy coming into your body as food equals the amount going out through activity and exercise, you are said to be in 'energy balance'.

Clearly, one of the methods of losing weight is simply to eat less. However, this has a number of disadvantages for those exercising regularly. Firstly, it is more difficult to eat a sufficient quantity of nutrients; secondly, tissue other than fat is lost, particularly with extreme weight loss diets. At the onset of a diet, 70% of weight loss is from water (*see* fig. 22), reducing to about 20% by the time a person has been dieting for two weeks. Fat loss speeds up as the diet is continued, changing from 25% of the total weight loss in the early days of a diet, to about 70% after two weeks. Protein loss increases from 5% to 15% in the same timescale.

Rather than crash dieting then, a better method is to improve the general quality of the diet. It is not just the amount of food, but the type of food which is important. High-energy foods (those with a lot of Calories, especially fat and alcohol) should be restricted, and these should be replaced with low-Calorie equivalents. The total amount of food may remain the same. It is important not to reduce the carbohydrate foods too much as these provide both the energy for exercise, and necessary amounts of fibre. It is more important to reduce the high-fat foods, and use a low-fat/high carbohydrate diet.

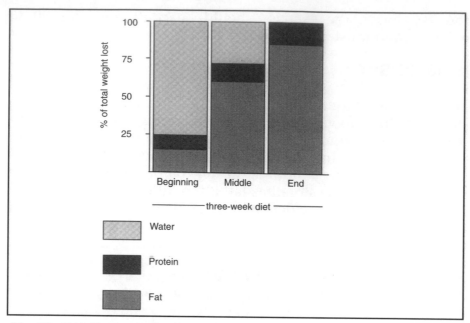

Fig.22 *Relative contributions of water, protein and fat to total weight lost during a three-week diet*

The essential items to restrict are alcohol, fast foods such as French fries and crisps, and snacks such as chocolate, because these are high in fat. Trim all visible fat and grill rather than fry food. Use less refined foods such as wholemeal bread and cereals, and eat starchy foods such as potatoes and pasta rather than sweet foods for energy.

CAN EXERCISE HELP YOU LOSE WEIGHT? • • • • • • • • • •

There are a number of myths about exercise and weight loss which we need to dispel. It is often said that if you start exercising your appetite will increase and you will put on weight. This is not so. Regular exercise helps to re-set the feeding control mechanism. Studies have shown that those who exercise regularly have a greater ability to accurately match the amount of food they want with the amount their body actually needs. This is especially important in children. Scientific studies have consistently shown that inactive children are more likely to be overweight in later life.

A second myth concerns the ability of exercise to burn off fat. You will hear people say that you would have to exercise all day to burn off the pounds they need to lose. After all, to lose just 1lb of bodyweight you would have to chop wood for 10 hours or play volleyball for 32 hours! However, this type of argument fails to take into account the regularity of exercise. Although only a small number of Calories are burned with each exercise bout, the cumulative effect is great. If, for example, you were to play two hours of golf, it would take four to five weeks to burn off 1lb of fat. But, if you play each week for the whole year, you will have burnt off nearly a stone in total – a very significant amount!

Coupling exercise with a good diet is the best route to permanent weight loss. As mentioned, exercise helps to re-set the feeding control mechanism, and the desire to eat too much is reduced. Secondly, exercise speeds up the metabolic rate – the 'ticking over' of the body, so that even when exercise has finished, energy will continue to be burned off. A half-hour workout, for example, will continue to burn up Calories for three or four hours afterwards. One of the important factors of course is that exercise will not just reduce weight but will increase muscle tone and add greatly to the overall improvement in physical appearance.

• • • • • • • • • • • • • • • • *KEYPOINT* • • • • • • • • • • • • • • • • •
Regular exercise is essential to effective, long-term weight loss.

BODYTYPE •

People often compare themselves to others to determine if they are satisfied with their body. Are they too big or too small, too fat or too thin? Is their waistline ok? Are their hips too big? Although this is understandable, one of the problems is that we each have a different bodytype. In other words, your body is unique, and the only way to really judge if you are in good shape is to know what feels and looks good for you.

The shape of the human body can be classified into three distinct types (*see* fig. 23). The first type is angular ('mesomorph'). This type of body tends to be muscular, with a typical 'Tarzan' appearance: the shoulders are broad and the waist is slim. These people tend to have large bones and thick-set muscles. The second type is more rounded ('endomorph') and represented by the 'Billy Bunter' shape. These individuals have a smooth, soft outline with a 'peardrop' appearance. The waist

Fig.23 Bodytypes: (a) Mesomorph – muscular; (b) Endomorph –
rounded; (c) Ectomorph – linear

and chest are often roughly the same measurement, and fat is
carried on the upper arms and thighs as well as around the
waist. The third type is linear ('ectomorph') represented by the
typical 'bean poles'. These individuals tend to be tall and thin,
with long legs and arms. Their muscles are long and fine, and
they have a wiry appearance.

In reality, we are all a mixture of these three extremes. But the
proportion of each bodytype you have will determine your
overall shape, and there is little you can do to change this.

Take as an example a young girl with a very rounded, stout
appearance. She sees models in the fashion magazines who are
tall and thin with long delicate limbs. Wanting to change her
appearance she joins a local aerobics class and starts dieting.
Initially her weight reduces but she becomes unhappy because
she feels she is not achieving what she wanted. She is fitter, and
her muscles are more toned, but she does not look like the
magazine models. Why? Not because she has failed to work
hard enough, but because she has a different bodytype. She has
a mixture of the rounded (endomorph) and angular (mesomorph) physiques, while the magazine model has a linear
(ectomorph) bodytype. This young girl is now fit and toned. She
should be happy, energetic and carefree. Instead she is
depressed and self-conscious because she is aiming to change
the bodytype she was born with. This is impossible. It is far

better to achieve the best you can for your own body than to want someone else's!

• • • • • • • • • • • • • • • *KEYPOINT* • • • • • • • • • • • • • • • •
Our bodies combine tendencies towards being fat, lean and muscled. The combination of these factors you were born with determines your bodytype.

DESIRABLE BODYWEIGHT • • • • • • • • • • • • • • • • • • •

We can receive some guidance about what bodyweight to aim at, providing we take into account our own bodytype. The charts in fig. 24 show desirable weights in relation to age, sex and frame size. When you are using these, make sure you weigh yourself at the same time each day to eliminate the effects of meals, and always wear the same type of clothing.

MEN Height in feet/inches	Small frame	Medium frame	Large frame
5.1	8.0–8.8	8.6–9.3	9.0–10.1
5.2	8.3–8.12	8.8–9.7	9.3–10.4
5.3	8.6–9.0	8.12–9.10	9.6–10.8
5.4	8.9–9.3	9.1–9.13	9.9–10.12
5.5	8.12–9.7	9.4–10.3	9.12–11.2
5.6	9.2–9.11	9.8–10.7	10.2–11.7
5.7	9.6–10.1	9.12–10.12	10.7–11.12
5.8	9.10–10.5	10.2–11.2	10.11–12.2
5.9	10.0–10.10	10.6–11.6	11.1–12.6
5.10	10.4–11.0	10.10–11.11	11.5–12.11
5.11	10.8–11.4	11.0–12.2	11.10–13.2
6.0	10.12–11.8	11.4–12.7	12.0–13.7
6.1	11.2–11.13	11.8–12.12	12.5–13.12
6.2	11.6–12.3	11.13–13.1	12.10–14.3
6.3	11.10–12.7	12.4–13.8	13.0–14.8
WOMEN Height in feet/inches	Small frame	Medium frame	Large frame
4.8	6.8–7.0	6.12–7.9	7.6–8.7
4.9	6.10–7.3	7.0–7.12	7.8–8.10
4.10	6.12–7.6	7.3–8.1	7.11–8.13
4.11	7.1–7.9	7.6–8.4	8.0–9.2
5.0	7.4–7.12	7.9–8.7	8.3–9.5
5.1	7.7–8.1	7.12–8.10	8.6–9.8
5.2	7.10–8.4	8.1–9.0	8.9–9.12
5.3	7.13–8.7	8.4–9.4	8.13–10.2
5.4	8.2–8.11	8.8–9.9	9.3–10.6
5.5	8.6–9.1	8.12–9.13	9.7–10.10
5.6	8.10–9.5	9.6–10.7	10.1–11.4
5.7	9.0–9.9	9.6–10.7	10.1–11.4
5.8	9.4–10.0	9.10–10.11	10.5–11.9
5.9	9.8–10.4	10.0–11.1	10.9–12.0
5.10	9.12–10.8	10.4–11.5	10.13–12.5

Fig.24 Bodyweight relative to height and frame size (stones/lbs)

The other method of checking your weight is to use the body mass index (B.M.I.). This is obtained by dividing your weight in kilograms (kg) by the square of your height in metres (m). For example, if you weigh 70 kg and you are 1.8 m tall, your B.M.I. is calculated as follows.

$$B.M.I. = \frac{weight\ (kg)}{height\ (m)\ squared}$$

$$= \frac{70}{1.8 \times 1.8} = 21.6$$

The B.M.I. is then classified from the table below.

> < 20 underweight
> 20–24.9 normal
> 25–29.9 overweight
> 30– 40 moderately obese
> 40+ severely obese

SUMMARY

• Bodyfat is more important than bodyweight. Your weight will include muscle, bone, tissues and fluids as well as fat.
• The feeding control mechanism (F.C.M.) in the brain attempts to match the amount of energy you take in as food to the amount you burn off through physical activity.
• Starches and sugars are energy-providing foods called carbo-hydrates.
• Fat is an energy store and is therefore high in Calories.
• Your basal metabolic rate (B.M.R.) is the 'tick-over rate' of your body.
• Physical exercise increases your body's tick-over, re-activates your feeding control mechanism, and increases muscle tone.
• You cannot substantially change the bodytype you were born with.

COMMON ABDOMINAL EXERCISES

One of the aims of the F.L.A.T. programme is to improve the standard of abdominal exercises, and in so doing to make exercises for this bodypart both safer and more effective. To fulfil this aim, the first thing we need to do is to take a close look at some commonly practised exercises and see where these go wrong. Although many of these have been practised for many years in numerous gyms and exercise classes there is still much room for improvement.

THE SIT-UP

The sit-up is often the first exercise turned to when abdominal training is considered. Unfortunately this exercise has a number of inherent dangers, especially for the spine. By knowing what happens to the body during this action we can reduce these dangers considerably.

Begin the exercise lying flat on your back. As soon as you lift your head from the floor, the abdominal muscles begin to work. This is because the muscles lifting the neck pull on the rib cage. To stop the ribs from moving, and hold them firm, the abdominal muscles must tighten. As the exercise continues, you begin to lift your trunk from the floor. To do this, your legs have to stay down. However, because your legs are lighter than your trunk, the tendency is always for the legs to lift unless the trunk is bent. Bending the trunk reduces the effect of leverage, and makes the trunk 'lighter'.

As an example of this mechanism study fig. 25. Two boys are sitting on a seesaw. The one on the right weighs 50 lbs (22 kg), but the boy on the left is heavier and weighs 60 lbs (27 kg). The seesaw is balanced at the moment, but if the lighter boy wants to lift the heavier boy, the heavier boy must move closer to the pivot point. This reduces his leverage effect and can be thought of as making him 'lighter'.

The same principle applies with the sit-up. If the trunk is to lift instead of the legs, the leverage effect of the trunk must be reduced. To do this the trunk must bend so that its weight moves closer to the hip which is acting as the pivot in this

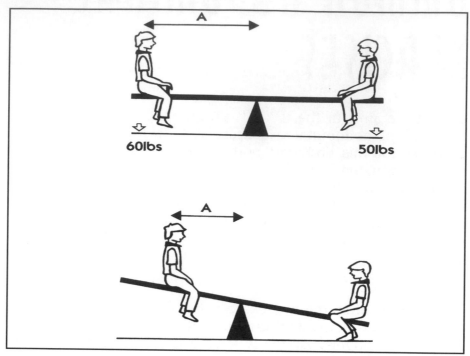

Fig.25 *Leverage. 'A' is the length of the lever which the heavier boy is using*

exercise (*see* fig. 26). If you are able to bend your trunk sufficiently, you will be able to sit up. But, if your abdominal muscles are weak or lengthened, your trunk will not bend enough to reduce its leverage, and so your trunk will stay on the ground and your legs will lift instead.

The abdominal muscles work to bend the trunk, but the lifting action which pulls the trunk away from the floor is carried out

▲   hip joint pivot
●   centre of gravity of upper body
▨   leverage

Fig.26 *Changing leverage in a sit-up*

Hip flexor muscle

a.

Direction of hip muscle pull

b.

c.

Direction of hip muscle pull

Fig.27 *(a) In the lying position the hip flexors pull parallel to the spine causing little lifting effect but maximal spinal compression; (b) when the hip flexors pull they can arch the spine; (c) bending the knees reduces spinal compression*

by the hip flexor muscles. These will pull hard on the spine to try to lift it up. If the legs are straight, the hip flexor muscles lie almost parallel to the spine (*see* fig. 27a). The muscles find it very difficult to lift the spine from this position, and instead they pull the lower spine into an arched position (*see* fig. 27b). If the knees and hips are bent (*see* fig. 27c), the hip flexor muscles are lifted up and they can now move the spine more easily and as a result will compress it less. Bending the hip therefore considerably reduces the stress on the lumbar spine.

• • • • • • • • • • • • • • • • **KEYPOINT** • • • • • • • • • • • • • • • • • •
Bending the legs in a sit-up reduces the unwanted forces on the lower back.

It must be emphasised that the stress on the spine from hip flexor action only occurs because the trunk is lifted clear of the ground. The action of lifting the trunk rather than simply curling it does not increase the work of the abdominals substantially, and is really unnecessary from the point of view of abdominal training. If the trunk stays on the ground, with the abdominals being used to bend the trunk only, the effects on the lumbar spine are reduced once again and the exercise becomes quite safe. This is why in the F.L.A.T. programme we use the trunk curl instead of the standard sit-up. It is more effective and far safer.

Fixing the feet during a sit-up enables you to pull harder with the hip flexor muscles. This in turn can increase the stress on the spine, and allow you to sit up without needing to bend your spine. The effect is therefore to increase the work of the hip flexors but reduce the work of the abdominals, precisely opposite to what we require from the exercise. In this programme we do not use foot fixation for basic abdominal exercises.

Inclining the sit-up bench changes the leverage effect on the spine (*see* fig. 28). In a normal sit-up (*see* fig. 28a) performed from the floor, the leverage acting on the trunk is maximum at the beginning of the exercise. As the trunk lifts, the leverage

Fig.28 *The inclined sit-up: (a) leverage reduces as movement continues; (b) leverage increases up to the mid-point of the movement*

reduces. If we incline the sit-up bench however (*see* fig. 28b), the leverage lessens at the beginning of the movement but increases to its maximum about half way through the exercise as the body moves into the horizontal position. As the trunk lifts further, it moves away from the horizontal and so the leverage forces reduce again. Inclining the bench makes the exercise harder therefore.

THE LEG RAISE ●

The leg raise can in some ways be seen as the reverse of the sit-up. With this exercise, the trunk stays on the ground and the legs are lifted instead. The movement now is purely from the hip flexors. They work to pull the legs up from the ground. However, again because the hip flexors lie parallel with the spine, they will tend to arch the lumbar spine and subject it to forces large enough to severely damage it. The problem occurs because as well as attaching to the lumbar spine, the hip flexors attach to the pelvis. As they pull, they will tend to tip the pelvis and pull the lumbar spine out of alignment. Normally the abdominal muscles will contract to stop this unwanted action occurring (*see* fig. 29a). If they are weak, however, the abdominals will be unable to do this and the pelvis will tilt, placing stress on the lumbar spine (*see* fig. 29b).

The problem can be greatly reduced if the legs are bent to reduce their leverage effect (*see* fig. 29c). The reduced leverage means that the abdominal muscles do not have to work as hard to hold the pelvis and lumbar spine in place. If they are weak, the abdominals may only be able to hold the pelvis still against the reduced leverage of the bent legs. In addition, if the hips are bent, the hip flexors can now pull at an angle rather than parallel to the spine. They will therefore compress the spine less, and be more effective in creating hip movement instead.

Leverage forces applied from the legs are greatest when the leg is horizontal. When performing this exercise therefore, we must keep the legs away from the horizontal. This can be achieved by performing the exercise against a wall with the legs beginning vertical. As the legs lower, the pelvis must be kept still. If it begins to tip, the exercise should stop because the abdominal muscles are failing to hold the pelvis stable. At this point, the legs are rested against the wall to take the weight off the spine. The movement is now to lower the legs from the vertical towards the wall rather than raising them from the floor.

53

Fig.29 *The leg raise: (a) as the hip flexor muscles pull on the pelvis, the abdominals stop the pelvis from tilting; (b) if the abdominals are weak, the pelvis tips forward, hollowing the lower back as the legs are lifted; (c) bending the knees reduces the leverage effect*

The same reservation applies with this exercise as with the sit-up. The hip flexors are working primarily, and the abdominals are holding the spine still. If we want to work the abdominals harder, we must modify the leg raise so that the spine bends and the tail lifts off the ground. This exercise is the 'pelvic raise', sometimes called the 'reverse crunch'. It is described on page 83 and forms an essential part of the F.L.A.T. programme.

• • • • • • • • • • • • • • • • *KEYPOINT* • • • • • • • • • • • • • • • • •
Do not allow the legs to move into a horizontal position when performing a leg raise action.

THE TRUNK CRUNCH •

The trunk crunch is a modification of the standard sit-up originally used by professional bodybuilders. As such it is an intense exercise and not suitable for the novice.

The exercise begins lying on the floor on your back. The knees and hips are bent to 90°, and the calves are placed on a bench or chair. From this position a sit-up is performed, moving the head towards the knees.

The exercise begins in the same way as the sit-up, with the abdominal muscles working hard. Because the pelvis remains still, the emphasis of the exercise is on the upper abdominals with the lower portion of the muscles showing less activity. As the spine bends maximally you reach a point where you must lift yourself up from the floor. In lighter subjects this may not be possible, but those who have heavier legs will be able to achieve this movement. Performing the action with the legs fixed enables you to pull the feet against the fixation point. As this happens the hip flexor muscles pull hard to lift the spine off the ground.

If the action is performed with a twist, the oblique abdominals will work more, but the central abdominal muscle (rectus abdominis) will still work hard.

Although a useful exercise because it strongly emphasises the upper portion of the abdominal muscles, it must be balanced out by using the pelvic raise to work the lower portion of the muscles. Failure to do this will leave an imbalance between the upper and lower portion of the abdominals, a situation which could lead to back pain.

The trunk crunch is not suitable for those who have suffered from back pain or those who require light training. It is included as an advanced exercise in the F.L.A.T. programme, performed with the feet not fixed to reduce stress on the lower spine. In the programme, use of the exercise is balanced by performing the pelvic raise in the same exercise session.

● ● ● ● ● ● ● ● ● ● ● ● ● ● ● ● **KEYPOINT** ● ● ● ● ● ● ● ● ● ● ● ● ● ● ● ●

The trunk crunch is an advanced exercise to be used only after initial abdominal strength has been gained using other exercises. The crunch focuses on the upper abdominal region, and must be balanced by movements which emphasise the lower abdominal area, such as the pelvic raise.

THE KNEE RAISE (HIP FLEXOR) ● ● ● ● ● ● ● ● ● ● ● ● ● ● ● ● ●

The hip flexor station is a standard attachment to many multi-gym weight training units and is often found in many commercial gym set-ups. The machine consists of a back pad and two side gutter pads to take the forearms.

Fig.30 *The knee raise: (a) the abdominals work to hold the pelvis firm at the beginning of the movement; (b) if the legs are allowed to swing backwards, the lower back will hollow dangerously (hyper-extend); (c) knees and hips bent to 90°; (d) trunk flexes to lift legs*

Normal instructions are to lift yourself up into the machine with your elbows bent to 90° and your forearms in the gutter pads (*see* fig. 30). The small of your back is pressed against the back pad. From this position lift your legs, keeping them straight, to the horizontal position and then lower them down again.

As the legs lift, the hip flexors work. To stabilise the spine and pelvis the abdominal muscles tighten. Only when the spine begins to bend, as the legs near the horizontal position, do the abdominals work to actively bend the spine. Although the exercise feels hard, the greatest amount of the work is from the hip flexors, with the abdominals receiving only a poor workout.

One of the major problems with this exercise stems from the length of the hamstring muscles on the back of the thigh. In many people these muscles are very short. When this is the case, you are not able to lift the legs out straight without the knees bending. If you try to hold the knees straight, the tight hamstrings will pull on the pelvis and cause the lower spine to bend. This can place stress on the spine.

A second area of concern is due to momentum. Because some people find the exercise hard, there is a tendency to swing the legs to assist the movement. When this happens, the momentum of the heavy legs moving at speed becomes uncontrollable. As the legs are lowered, they swing backwards forcing the back to hyperextend (*see* fig. 30b) and severely stressing the spine.

The hip flexor exercise can be made safer and more effective with some modifications. Firstly, the knees should be bent to relax the hamstrings and so reduce the stress on the lower back. In addition, bending the knees reduces the leverage effect and makes the exercise more controllable. If the knees are bent to 90° and kept still, the action can then be one of bending the trunk to pull the tailbone away from the pad (*see* fig. 30c). This increases the emphasis on the abdominal muscles, making the exercise more effective. Secondly, any swinging of the legs should be avoided. As the legs are lowered they should be under control. In the bottom position, pause before you start to lift the legs again. In this way momentum is cut down and the back is not forced into an unnatural position.

•••••••••••••••••• *KEYPOINT* ••••••••••••••••••
The knee raise can place stress on the lower back if it is performed with a 'swinging' action. Keep the action under control at all times, especially when lowering the legs.

TRUNK EXERCISE DANGERS

More than any other area in the body, the back is susceptible to injury through incorrect exercise. To prevent injury, we need to have an understanding of some basic mechanical concepts.

LEVERAGE •

The limbs and spine act as levers when we move. A lever is simply a rigid bar which moves around a fixed point or pivot. Two forces act on the lever: effort and resistance. The effort tries to move the lever, while the resistance tries to stop movement. In the body, the effort is supplied by your muscles, while the resistance is the weight of the bodypart. Take as an example the leg lifting from a lying position. The pivot is the hip joint, the effort is supplied by the hip flexor muscles which lift the leg, and the resistance is the weight of the whole leg. The effort from the muscle acts at the point where the muscle attaches to the thighbone (*see* fig. 31b).

We say that the weight acts through a single point called the 'centre of gravity'. This is really the balance point of the limb, and would be the centre point of the limb if the limb were the same size all over. However, because the leg is thicker at the top, the centre of gravity lies towards the heavier end.

Leverage is greater when there is a long horizontal distance between the pivot and the point where the weight or effort acts. In the example above, the leverage is greatest when the leg first lifts from the ground, because it is close to the horizontal. As the leg lifts up, it moves away from the horizontal and so the leverage reduces and the exercise actually gets easier. In fig. 31c the subject is standing up with the legs in the vertical position. The leverage to begin with is minimal. As the leg lifts, however, it moves towards the horizontal and so the leverage increases. This is now the reverse situation to fig. 31a, and the exercise gradually gets harder. Although both exercises involve flexing the straight leg, the starting position of the movement changes the effect of the exercise considerably.

Fig.31 *Leverage: (a) leverage reducing; (b) the leg as a lever; (c) leverage increasing*

59

> • • • • • • • • • • • • • • • • • **KEYPOINT** • • • • • • • • • • • • • • • • • •
> Leverage is greatest when a lever is in a horizontal position.

This example has important implications with regard to the safety of the spine. Exercises which involve moving the spine into a horizontal position will place great amounts of leverage on the spine and should be used with caution. Often, simply altering the starting position will move the spine away from the horizontal and so reduce the stress on the lower back. Where a horizontal position must be used, the spine should be supported. As an example of this process let's look at a common stretch for the hamstring muscles on the back of the thigh. In fig. 32a an athlete is stretching the hamstrings by bending the trunk forwards from the hip. This action places an excessive leverage stress on the spine because it is moving from a vertical position (minimal leverage) to a more horizontal position (maximum leverage). Simply by placing one hand down on the knee, the spine is supported and the stress reduced (*see* fig. 32b).

Fig.32 *Supporting the body when leverage is large: (a) spine moves towards the horizontal, leverage increases; (b) bodyweight taken through the arm at the point of maximum leverage*

• • • • • • • • • • • • • • • • *KEYPOINT* • • • • • • • • • • • • • • • • •
If an exercise doesn't allow you to keep your spine vertical,
place your hand on something for support.

WHICH BODY AREA IS MOVING? • • • • • • • • • • • • • • • • • • •

Often, a quick look at an exercise creates the impression that a particular part of the body is moving. On closer inspection, however, it can be seen that other body areas are also moving and these may be taking greater stress than was intended. This holds true particularly with the pelvis moving on the spine or hip. Take as an example a stretch for the thigh muscles (*see* fig. 33). The subject is standing up straight and has grasped the ankle. They are pulling the hip backwards and trying to increase the bend on the knee at the same time. At first sight this seems to be an exercise which is simply placing stretch on the thigh muscles. However, if we look closely we can see that the pelvis has tilted forwards and stress is now placed on the spine. In this case the spine is more flexible than the tight thigh muscles, so the more the stretch is pushed, the more stress is thrown on to the spine.

Fig.33 (a) Normal pelvic tilt and lower back alignment; (b) pelvis moves excessively, causing lower back to hollow. Leg goes higher, but technique is faulty

If we look at fig. 34, the subjects are trying to touch their toes by stretching their hamstrings behind the thigh. The subject in fig. 34b appears to be stretching further because they have reached closer to their toes. However, if we look at the line of the pelvis, both individuals have moved exactly the same amount. The extra movement in fig. 34b has occurred by overbending the upper spine. Again, this part of the body is generally more flexible than the tight hamstrings. As the movement is pushed further and further, the stretch on the hamstrings will not increase, but the stress on the upper spine certainly will.

Fig.34 *(a) Normal movement; (b) excessive movement of upper spine*

•••••••••••••••• **KEYPOINT** ••••••••••••••••
Looking at the pelvis gives an important indication of lumbar spine position.

MOMENTUM ●

Momentum is a combination of how heavy an object is and how quickly it is moving. A heavy object, such as the leg or trunk, which is moving quickly, will possess a great deal of momentum and will be very difficult to stop. The high momentum can take over the movement, and you may find that you are no longer able to control a bodypart. This is when injuries can occur.

There are two methods to make this type of exercise safer. Firstly, you can reduce the momentum by slowing the movement down where heavy bodyparts are used. In the programme, all movements of the trunk are slow to begin with. It is only when we have a considerable degree of control over an action that speed is increased.

The second way to make a movement safer, if it is moving quickly, is to ensure that the movement only occurs in the middle of the joint range. The joint range is the total movement from one extreme to the other (*see* page 8). In the case of the knee, it would be from the fully bent position to fully straight. Where an action is rapid, we must restrict the movement to the middle part of this range so that the joint is never fully bent or fully straightened. In this way we reduce the likelihood of injuring the joint tissues by overstretching them.

> ● ● ● ● ● ● ● ● ● ● ● ● ● ● ● *KEYPOINT* ● ● ● ● ● ● ● ● ● ● ● ● ● ● ● ●
> Keep movements slow and controlled. Use the middle of a
> joint's total movement more often than the ends.

EXCESSIVE LUMBAR CURVATURE ● ● ● ● ● ● ● ● ● ● ● ● ● ● ●

We have seen earlier that pelvic tilt is intimately linked with lumbar curvature. Tilting the pelvis forwards increases the lumbar curve, while tilting it backwards flattens it. One of the aims of this programme is to enable a subject to identify the neutral position of the spine, where the pelvis is level, and to hold this position while performing other movements.

If the pelvis is allowed to tilt too far, the lumbar spine will move to its end point. At this point the disc, spinal facet joints and lumbar tissues are all stressed excessively. Increasing the curve will press the facet joints together, while flattening the curve will push the spinal disc backwards. In each case the ligaments surrounding the spinal tissues are overstretched.

A number of abdominal exercises will tend to dangerously increase the lumbar curve. In the straight leg raise action (*see* fig. 35a), the pull of the hip muscles on to the pelvis and lumbar spine tends to tilt the pelvis forwards and lift the lumbar spine away from the ground. Even if the spine remains flat on the floor, the hip muscles still pull dangerously hard on to the lower spine, compressing the discs and increasing the likelihood of injury. The safer alternative to this exercise is the heel slide (*see* page 78). Now only one leg is lifting at a time, the other one remaining on the floor to provide support and increase stability. In addition, the heel of the leg which moves stays on the ground so the full weight is not lifted.

With spinal hyperextension exercises in an unsupported position (*see* fig. 35b), the abdominal muscles may be unable to support the spine and hold it in its neutral position. As a consequence the pelvis tilts forwards and the lumbar spine moves too far into extension. As we have seen, this position compresses the joints in the base of the spine. This compression is compounded by the powerful contraction of the spinal extensor muscles which are fighting to hold the body up. Alternatives to this exercise include bridging (*see* page 87) and the spinal extension hold (*see* page 100). In each case the whole bodyweight is not taken until all the trunk muscles are strong enough to do this. When the muscles are strong, the pelvis is aligned and the abdominal hollowing procedure is practised first, before the exercise begins. In this way the spine is correctly aligned before it is loaded.

Overhead pressing actions in weight training can also lead to hyperextension of the lumbar spine through the pelvis tilt mechanism if the abdominal muscles fail to contract at the onset of the lift (*see* fig. 35c). To prevent this happening, firstly the abdominal hollowing procedure must be practised throughout the lift. Secondly, the limiting factor should not be the amount of weight that can be lifted overhead, but the point at which the pelvis begins to tilt. When this happens, the exercise must stop, however large or small the weight being lifted.

Flattening of the lumbar spine is common in sitting positions. Squatting on to a bench which is too low, for example (*see* fig. 35d), will allow the pelvis to tilt backwards and this in turn pulls the spinal bones into a flexed position. Done at speed, this type of action can be extremely dangerous. The movement can be modified in two ways. Firstly, the bench height must be adjusted so that it is just higher than the subject's knee. In this way the amount of knee and hip movement is reduced and the lumbar spine will not be rounded as far. Secondly, the movement should be slowed down so that the momentum is reduced. In this way, less stress is passed on to the spine, and the action stays controlled all the time.

Fig.35 *Excessive lumbar curvature*

> • • • • • • • • • • • • • • • *KEYPOINT* • • • • • • • • • • • • • • • • •
> Try to keep your spine in the neutral position as often as
> possible.

NECK POSTURE •

In an earlier section we saw that the posture line can be used to
determine optimal posture. With reference to the head and neck,
the posture line should pass through the shoulder joint and also
through the ear. A common faulty alignment seen in exercise is
where the head is held forward (*see* fig. 36a). The ear can be seen
to move about 2–4 in (5–10 cm) forwards of the posture line and
well in front of the shoulder. This stresses the neck tissues and is
very dangerous when performed at speed. The movement is
common when the head is used to lead, and provides momentum to get an action started. This is especially true of sit-up type
exercises. If a subject is attempting to sit up from the ground,
they may be unable to do so if their abdominal muscles are very
weak. One way that they can cover this up is to perform the
action quickly and use the weight of the head to 'fling' the body
off the ground (*see* fig. 36b). This rapid action can damage the
neck structures sufficiently to cause a trapped nerve and even a
type of whiplash injury.

a.

b.

Fig.36 *Neck position: (a) correct (left); too far forward (right);*
(b) placing the hands behind the head during a sit-up forces the
head forwards and stresses the neck. The dotted figure shows the
correct alignment

To avoid this neck posture, the chin should be held back, in alignment with the rest of the spine. This position is held so the head does not move, and the action is performed slowly, under control.

•••••••••••••••• **KEYPOINT** ••••••••••••••••••

Avoid nodding your head when performing abdominal exercises.

STABILITY ••••••••••••••••••••••••••••••••

Three factors are important to stability: the size and alignment of the base of support, and the centre of gravity. An object's base of support is the total area that is on the ground or, in the case of the human body, the distance between the feet (*see* fig. 37). If the base of support is wide, the weight of the object is distributed over a large area and the object is therefore stable, like a pyramid. When the base of support is small, as with a ballet dancer *en point*, the object is unstable and likely to wobble off balance. When choosing an exercise position, therefore, we should make sure that our base of support is as wide as is comfortable.

The second factor concerning the base of support which is important to stability is the direction in which it faces. Aligning your feet so that they face the way you are moving makes you more stable. For example, if you have your feet one in front of the other, although your base of support is large, you will still be unstable if you are practising a side bend movement. This is because the side bend movement occurs in a side-to-side direction, but your feet position has widened your base of support in a forward-to-back direction. To be stable while performing side bends your feet must be apart in a sideways direction. Similarly, if your feet are apart sideways you are unstable when performing shoulder rounding and bracing. This movement occurs front-to-back, so your base of support should be widened in this direction.

The third factor which is important to stability is the height of your bodyweight above the ground. When you stand tall, you are less stable and there is a tendency to topple when performing exercises. Simply bending your knees lowers your bodyweight closer to the ground and makes you more stable.

Fig.37 Stability: (a) black area is the base of support – stable when wide; (b) unstable – small base of support; (c) base is wide in direction of movement – stable; (d) base is widened in direction different to movement – less stable

> • • • • • • • • • • • • • • • • **KEYPOINT** • • • • • • • • • • • • • • • • •
> To make yourself more stable, keep your feet apart and face
> the direction of travel. Bend your knees slightly.

COMFORT •

An exercise which is uncomfortable can also be dangerous.
When you are not comfortable you tend to alter your posture
regularly, and wriggle. This takes concentration away from the
exercise and affects stability. An exercise usually becomes
uncomfortable if you are placing weight through a bony point
such as the knee, hip or tailbone, and pressure builds up. In each
of these cases try to rest the bodypart on a mat or folded towel
instead of on the floor alone.

Taking up an unnatural posture will also make you uncomfortable as it will stress the body tissues excessively. When
using equipment, therefore, make sure it is adjusted to suit your
body size. This is especially true of weight training apparatus
where correct seat height adjustment is vital to allow correct
spinal alignment.

SUMMARY

• The centre of gravity of an object is its balance point.
• In a lever, the further away from the pivot a weight is placed,
the greater the leverage effect.
• Momentum is a combination of how heavy an object is and
how fast it is moving.
• Tilting the pelvis forwards *increases* the lumbar curve; tilting it
backwards *decreases* it.
• Stability is determined by the size and alignment of an object's
base of support and the position of its centre of gravity.

Before we start

WARM-UP •

Before we begin exercising we need to consider a few things in preparation.

The body takes time to change from its resting 'tick-over' to a point where it is ready to face the rigours of intense exercise. Just as a car needs to be warmed up before it will run smoothly, so the body must speed up gradually to be at its best. When you are cold, your body tissues are stiffer and less pliable. This means that your joints and muscles can be damaged more easily. In order to reduce the likelihood of injury and make exercise more effective, we need to practise a warm-up.

A warm-up can either be 'passive', where the body is heated from the outside, or 'active', where exercise is used to form the heat internally. An example of a passive warm-up is to have a hot shower or sauna, while an active warm-up can be achieved by gentle jogging, for example. Both types of warm-up can be effective, but are appropriate to different situations. An active warm-up is the type normally used before general exercise, while a passive warm-up is useful when you may be recovering from an injury, and it would not be safe to practise vigorous exercise.

To be effective, a warm-up should be intense enough to cause mild sweating. Gentle jogging, light aerobics, or cycling on an exercise bicycle, are all good warm-up activities. The joints should be taken through their full range of movement, starting with small movements, gradually becoming larger. Slowly circle the arms, twist the spine, and bend the legs until all the major joints have been worked. The emphasis is on slow, controlled movements which do not stress the body, but which prepare it for activity.

Following exercise, you will need to warm down by reducing your activity slowly, rather than with a sudden jolt. This will have the additional benefit of reducing muscle ache.

Comfort

Clothing should be warm to maintain bodyheat, and loose-fitting to allow unrestricted movement. Shorts and a T-shirt are fine for warmer weather, but fleecy jog bottoms and a sweatshirt are normally better when it is cooler. Remember that you may need to see your spine in the mirror at some stage of the exercise programme, so try to wear layers of clothing which you can gradually remove.

Make sure that you can move without restriction from furniture or other people. A little time spent clearing some space in the room you are going to exercise in is well worthwhile. You may need a small exercise mat or a number of folded towels to hand for padding during exercises where you are kneeling or lying on the floor.

•••••••••••••••• *KEYPOINT* ••••••••••••••••••
Wear comfortable clothing, and warm up gradually before you
begin the F.L.A.T. programme.

FOUNDATION

We begin the programme by mastering two essential move-ments. These form the cornerstones of F.L.A.T. and are often used as parts of other more advanced exercises later in the programme. The foundation movements are important because they involve re-learning important skills relating to control of spinal movement which have often been forgotten. Were you to try to perform abdominal exercises before you have mastered these skills, your movement control would be so poor that injury may result. Time spent on the foundation exercises is therefore a sound investment for the future.

Because the foundation movements are practising *skills*, they should be used regularly throughout the day rather than simply during an exercise programme.

PELVIC TILTING

We saw on page 9 that the tilt of the pelvis determines the position of the lower back. Tilting the pelvis forwards increases the hollow in the small of the back, while tilting the pelvis back-wards flattens the back, reducing the lumbar hollow. The reason pelvic tilting is so important is that it teaches control of the lumbar spine during exercise. An incorrect pelvic tilt during exercise can lead to excessive movement in the lower spine. We must be able to identify this when it is happening, by feeling the action taking place, so that we can correct it before an injury occurs. Because accurate control of this action is so vital, we practise the movement from two different starting positions.

PELVIC TILTING IN LYING

■ Starting position
Begin lying on your back with your knees bent. Place your feet and knees shoulder width apart. Your arms should rest on the floor slightly away from your body.

■ Action
Tighten your abdominal muscles and your buttock muscles to tip your pelvis backwards and flatten the small of your back against the floor. Pause and then reverse the action, tightening your back and hip muscles to hollow the small of your back away from the floor. Repeat this action and try to stop the movement when you are half way between the two extremes. *This mid-point is your neutral position.*

■ Points to note
The pelvic tilting action should be brought about by contraction of the abdominal muscles and buttock muscles together. Although it is possible to perform the action with one set of muscles alone, working both sets will give you more control.

■ Training tip
The action must be smooth and controlled rather than jerky. A jerking action will stress the lower spine.

PELVIC TILTING IN STANDING

■ Starting position
Begin standing with your feet shoulder width apart, arms by your sides. Stand tall. Do not slouch.

■ Action
Tighten your abdominal muscles and your buttock muscles together to tilt your pelvis backwards and flatten your lower spine. Pause and then tighten your hips and spinal muscles to increase the hollow in the small of your back.

■ Points to note
The action should be isolated to your lower back. Your shoulders should stay square, and your knees should remain still. Avoid any body sway.

■ Training tip
Placing your hands out to the side in a 'T' shape will help with the balance of this exercise, and make any unwanted body sway more obvious.

ABDOMINAL HOLLOWING •

We saw on pages 13 and 14 that the transversus abdominis is an important muscle to maintain stability of the lower spine. This muscle is often not used in exercise programmes, but it is vital that we work it before we move on to further abdominal training. The muscle works hard during the abdominal hollowing actions described below. Even if you have been training for many years, practise this movement because you may be surprised at just how little control you have in this body area.

ABDOMINAL HOLLOWING IN KNEELING

■ Starting position
Begin kneeling on all fours with your hands and knees shoulder width apart. Kneel on a mat or folded towel for comfort.

■ Action
Allow your tummy muscles to relax and sag downwards to the floor. Then tighten them and pull them up and in, trying to hollow your tummy.

■ Points to note
Initially the amount of movement may be very small, but with practice you should notice 4–6 in (10–15 cm) of movement in total. Breathe normally throughout the action; do not take a deep breath when trying to flatten your tummy. Keep your spine still as you hollow. Do not arch the spine or tilt the pelvis.

■ Training tip
Place a mirror on the floor beneath your tummy so you can see what is happening. Focus your attention on your tummy button, and try to move it rather than the whole of your abdomen.

ABDOMINAL HOLLOWING IN SITTING

■ Starting position
Sit on a stool with your knees apart. Sit tall with your back slightly hollow. Place one hand on your tummy and the other in the small of your back.

■ Action
Perform the abdominal hollowing action by pulling your tummy in and up away from your front hand, focusing your attention on your tummy button.

■ Points to note
When sitting, try to sit tall, rather than slouching or holding the trunk too rigid.

■ Training tip
Use your hands to monitor the neutral position of your spine and also to give you feedback about the abdominal hollowing action.

ABDOMINAL HOLLOWING IN STANDING

■ Starting position
Stand upright with your feet shoulder width apart. Place your lower spine in its neutral position.

■ Action
Perform the abdominal hollowing action by focusing on your tummy button and pulling it in and up.

■ Points to note
Breathe normally throughout the movement; do not hold your breath. Make sure that your spine, hips and legs stay still. Isolate the movement to your tummy alone; do not flatten your back or tilt your pelvis.

■ Training tip
Begin by practising this exercise standing side-on to a mirror. Place a belt loosely around your lower tummy. As you hollow, a gap should form between your tummy and the belt.

Level One

Heel slide ●

▪ Starting position

Begin lying on the floor on your back. Your feet and knees should be 4–6 in (10–15 cm) apart. Put your hands on your tummy, with the heel of the hand over your pelvic bones. Place the heel of each foot on a shiny piece of paper on a carpet, or a soft cloth on a hard wooden floor.

▪ Action

Perform the abdominal hollowing action and hold the abdomen tight. Feel the muscles tense beneath your fingers. Continue to breathe normally throughout the exercise. Slide one leg out straight while holding your tummy tight. As soon as the heel of your hand feels your pelvis begin to tip, slide the leg back in again.

▪ Points to note

The aim of this exercise is to build up the ability of the abdominal muscles to hold the pelvis firm. The action of the leg muscles is therefore secondary to that of the abdominals.

▪ Training tip

The weight of your leg should be taken by the floor throughout the movement. Do not lift your heel up from the ground. The action is to *slide*, not to lift.

LEG SHORTENING (LYING) ●

■ Starting position
Begin lying on the floor on your back with your feet 8 in (20 cm) apart. Place your arms out sideways in a 'T' shape.

■ Action
Tip your pelvis from side to side ('hitching the hip') to firstly shorten and then lengthen each leg.

■ Points to note
The leg must remain perfectly straight to focus the movement on the pelvis, and through this on to the lower spine.

■ Training tip
Flex your foot, and lead the movement with your heel.

TRUNK CURL SEQUENCE • • • • • • • • • • • • • • • • • •

1. Pelvic tilt
2. Hollowing
3. Fingers to heels

■ Starting position

Begin lying on your back with your knees bent. Your feet should be shoulder width apart.

■ Action

Perform the pelvic tilt and flatten your back on to the floor. Next, perform the abdominal hollowing action, pulling your tummy button in. Finally, reach forwards with your fingers towards your heels so that your trunk bends and your shoulders lift away from the floor.

■ Points to note

The action of this exercise is to *bend the trunk*, not to sit up. The bottom part of the shoulder blades should stay in contact with the ground throughout the movement. As you perform the abdominal hollowing action, breathe out. Breathe in as you release the movement.

■ Training tip

Reaching forwards (along the ground) towards the heels rather than upwards for the knees, encourages the correct trunk bending action.

ABDOMINAL HOLLOWING WITH GLUTEAL BRACE ● ● ● ● ● ●

■ Starting position
Begin lying on your front on the floor. Tuck your feet under so your toes are flexed. Place a folded towel beneath your forehead for comfort.

■ Action
Perform the abdominal hollowing action by pulling your tummy in tight, focusing your attention on your tummy button. At the same time, tighten your buttocks and brace your legs out straight.

■ Points to note
You must maintain the neutral position of your spine throughout the action. Make sure you don't tilt your pelvis forwards or backwards.

■ Training tip
Tighten your tummy first, and then grip your buttocks together. Once you have mastered the individual actions, try performing both at the same time.

'X' TONE •

■ Starting position

Begin lying on the floor on your back with your knees bent, feet flat. Your knees and feet should be about 8–12 in (20–30 cm) apart.

■ Action

Reach past the outside of your right knee with your left hand. At the same time, lift your right foot off the ground and pull the right side of your pelvis towards you. Pause, and then reverse the action, reaching to the left.

■ Points to note

The aim of this exercise is to tone the oblique abdominals. To achieve this, the lower part of the trunk must take part in the action, so the hip pull is essential to the exercise.

■ Training tip

To emphasise the hip pull action, initially ask someone to press on to your hip as you pull. This will make isolating the action easier. *Remember to lift only one hip at a time!*

Level two

Pelvic raise (1) ● ● ● ● ● ● ● ● ● ● ● ● ● ● ● ● ● ● ●

■ Starting position
Begin lying on the floor on your back. Your arms should rest on the floor by your sides (palms down) making an angle of 45° to your body. Bend your knees and draw them up on to your chest.

■ Action
Bend your spine to lift your tailbone 1 in (3 cm) off the ground, at the same time pulling your knees upwards towards your shoulders.

■ Points to note
Do not lunge into the movement using the momentum of your legs. The action should be a gentle raising of the lower spine, with the power of the trunk muscles lifting the inactive legs.

■ Training tip
Press down hard with your straight arms on to the floor as you flex your lower spine.

BENCH CRUNCH •

■ Starting position
Begin lying on the floor on your back. Place your calves on a low chair or stool so that your knees and hips are bent to 90°. Your feet and knees should be 8–12 in (20–30 cm) apart.

■ Action
Sit forwards, as though trying to touch your chest flat on to your thighs.

■ Points to note
This is an advanced exercise and as such you may not be able to lift forwards very far to begin with. Do not speed the movement up in an attempt to sit up further. This will simply increase the momentum of your trunk but will not work the abdominal muscles harder.

■ Training tip
Try to bend your trunk as you begin to sit forwards, to shorten the abdominal muscles.

OBLIQUE BENCH CRUNCH ●

Do not attempt this exercise until you can comfortably perform ten repetitions of the bench crunch.

■ Starting position
Begin lying on the floor on your back. Place your calves on a low chair or stool so that your knees and hips are bent to 90°. Your feet and knees should be 8–12 in (20–30 cm) apart. Fold your arms lightly, keeping your elbows bent to 90°.

■ Action
Sit up, and at the same time reach your right elbow past your left knee. Pause and then repeat the action, reaching with your left elbow past your right knee.

■ Points to note
As with the bench crunch, make sure that the exercise is performed slowly, under control. A rapid action will enable you to sit up further, but only through momentum.

■ Training tip
Exhale hard as you sit up, but rest after each pair of oblique crunches, and breathe normally so you do not get dizzy.

KNEE ROLLING •

■ Starting position
Lie on your back with your knees bent, feet flat on the floor.
Place your arms out sideways in a 'T' shape to aid stability.

■ Action
Perform the abdominal hollowing action, and hold the tummy
muscles tight throughout the movement. Allow the knees to
slowly lower to one side, forming an angle of about 30° to the
vertical. Pull the knees back to the mid-position and then repeat
the action.

■ Points to note
Breathe normally throughout the exercise; do not hold your
breath. Make sure you keep both hips on the ground as you
lower the knees.

■ Training tip
If you cannot lower your knees to the ground, place a cushion
on the floor at either side of your hips. Lower your knees on to
the cushion rather than right down on to the floor to begin with.

Bridging ●

■ Starting position
Begin lying on your back with your knees bent and feet flat on the floor. Your feet should be shoulder width apart. Find your neutral position and maintain this throughout the exercise.

■ Action
Perform the abdominal hollowing action and then tighten your buttock muscles and lift your hips 4 in (10 cm) from the floor.

■ Points to note
The lower spine must stay in its neutral position, so make sure that you don't lift too high or your spine will arch. Your tummy and upper leg should be in line.

■ Training tip
Allow the squeeze of the buttock muscles to lead the movement and lift you, rather than leading with your stomach.

LEVEL THREE

PELVIC RAISE (2) ●

You must be able to perform 5–10 repetitions of pelvic raise (1) before attempting this exercise.

■ Starting position
Begin lying on the floor on your back. Your arms should rest on the floor by your sides (palms down), making an angle of 45° to your body. Bend your knees and hips to 90°.

■ Action
Bend your spine to lift your tailbone 1 in (3 cm) off the ground, while holding your hips still.

■ Points to note
This exercise works the lower abdominals hard. However, work is taken off these muscles if rapid hip flexion is used to lever the spine off the floor. The hips should stay inactive throughout the movement, with the power of the exercise coming from the lower abdominals only. Keep the knees off the chest.

■ Training tip
Press down hard with your straight arms on to the floor as you flex your lower spine. Begin by lifting the tailbone and then the last spinal bone followed by the next to last.

SIDE BEND IN SIDE LYING ● ● ● ● ● ● ● ● ● ● ● ● ● ● ● ● ● ●

■ Starting position
Begin lying on your side on a mat. Bend your lower arm and leg slightly to improve your stability. Rest your head lightly on your hand for support.

■ Action
Perform a side-bending action so that your lower shoulder lifts from the floor by ¾ in (2 cm). At the same time, 'hitch' your upper leg so that you shorten it by ¾ in (2 cm).

■ Points to note
The total side-bend movement is very small, so neither the trunk nor the leg should lift very far.

■ Training tip
Imagine you are 'gathering' the skin at the side of the trunk as your trunk pulls in one direction and your leg in the other.

ROPE CLIMB ●

Do not attempt this exercise until you can perform ten repetitions of the trunk curl and bench crunch comfortably.

■ Starting position
Begin lying on the floor with your knees bent, arms by your sides. Your feet and knees should be 8–10 in (20–30 cm) apart.

■ Action
Imagine a line joining your knees, and focus on a point just above the centre of this line. Reach up with your right hand for this point by curling and twisting your trunk. Pause and then allow yourself to sit back down partially. Immediately reach up with the other hand to the same point, and then continue to repeat the action.

■ Points to note
The lower spine should stay on the ground; only the chest and shoulders lift up. Keep the trunk curled throughout the movement so that you maintain tension in the abdominal muscles. Breathe normally throughout the movement, *do not* hold your breath.

■ Training tip
As you reach towards the high point in this movement, grip as though you are pulling on a rope. As you lower down, keep reaching forwards with your arm to maintain the curled position of the trunk.

Negative crunch •

Do not attempt this exercise until you can perform ten repetitions of the trunk crunch comfortably.

■ Starting position
Begin lying on a mat on your back. Place your calves on a low chair or stool so that your knees and hips are bent to 90°. Your feet and knees should be 8–12 in (20–30 cm) apart. Fix your feet by hooking them under an object or ask a training partner to hold them firmly.

■ Action
Reach forwards and grip your knees. Pull yourself up using just arm strength until your chest touches your thighs. Flex your trunk so your head touches your knees, and maintain this flexed position throughout the exercise. Slowly lower your upper body back down on to the floor inch by inch, taking a total of 30 seconds to complete the movement.

■ Points to note
Make sure you breathe normally throughout the movement; *do not* hold your breath.

■ Training tip
Make sure your tail touches the floor first, followed by the small of your back, the mid-back, shoulder blades and finally the shoulders themselves.

STRAIGHT LEG ROLL •

Do not attempt this exercise until you can perform ten repetitions of knee rolling comfortably.

■ Starting position
Lie on the floor with your knees bent. Stretch your arms out to the side in a 'T' shape to aid stability. Draw your knees up on to your chest and then straighten your legs so that your hips, knees and feet are in line.

■ Action
Gradually lower your legs, keeping them straight, sideways on to the floor. Keep the arms and shoulders pressed tightly against the floor for stability.

■ Points to note
The hips remain on the floor as the trunk twists. Make sure the action stays controlled. *Do not* allow the legs to rapidly drop to the floor.

■ Training tip
When you begin the exercise, place two cushions on the floor at either side of your hips. Start the exercise by lowering your legs on to the cushions rather than the floor.

ABDOMINAL TRAINING IN SPORT

The principles which make up the F.L.A.T. programme may be used in sport in two ways. Firstly, the exercises described earlier may be incorporated into a general training programme. This will have the effect of making the trunk section of any training programme far safer and more effective. In addition, because the arms and legs depend on the stability of the trunk to push and pull from, the function of the limbs may well improve. The final way in which the programme can contribute is by using the underlying principle of ensuring trunk stability as a foundation for other movements in all sports actions. In this way we can modify commonly used exercises to improve them.

WEIGHT TRAINING

We have seen that the neutral position of the spine should be maintained as often as possible to reduce stress acting on the lumbar region. One of the ways of doing this and of stabilising the spine is to practise the abdominal hollowing action. By pulling the abdominal muscles in tightly, the trunk becomes more stable and body alignment is improved. In fig. 38a, the athlete is performing a shoulder press action. The pelvis has tipped forwards and the lumbar curve has become excessive. By tightening the abdominal muscles (see fig. 38b), the pelvis will remain level and the lumbar spine is correctly aligned. In addition, the athlete in fig. 38b has widened the base of support and is therefore more stable. The combination of stable spine and stable base makes the exercise far safer.

The same applies to fig. 39. Initially, the athlete performing the arm curl has allowed the pelvis to tip forwards and is dangerously overextending the spine to swing the weight upwards. In fig. 39b, by modifying the exercise using the programme's principles, the exercise is far safer. Firstly, abdominal hollowing has been used to correct the pelvic tilt and give the athlete a stable trunk to work from. Secondly, the base of support has been widened by placing the feet one in front of the other, and the knees are bent so that the legs, rather than the spine, give the spring to the action.

93

Fig.38 *Shoulder press: (a) stress on lower spine – unstable position; (b) spine correctly aligned – more stable postion*

Fig.39 *Arm curl: (a) back arching, spine dangerously overextended; (b) feet apart, spine aligned, abdominals tight*

In fig. 40 the athlete is performing a squat exercise. There are a number of errors in technique here which are making the exercise quite dangerous to the spine. Firstly, the pelvis has tipped right forwards, allowing the abdominal muscles to lengthen and protrude. This increases the lumbar curve and fails to stabilise the spine. In addition, the knees are not bent sufficiently to lower the weight. Instead the athlete has tipped the trunk forwards on the hip and allowed the spine to move forwards of the ideal posture line. The weight has been pulled forwards, and the leverage (measured as the distance between the weight and the posture line) has increased dramatically. By applying the F.L.A.T. principles with regard to spinal stability and posture, the exercise has been modified in fig. 40b. The athlete has corrected his posture by bending the knees more (the ankles are raised on a block). This has lowered the weight while keeping the spine and weight close to the posture line. The pelvis is level and the abdominal muscles have been pulled tight by performing the abdominal hollowing action. The spine is therefore more stable and less likely to be injured through excessive joint movement.

Fig.40 *Squat exercise: (a) pelvis tipped forwards, increased lumbar curvature, knees not bent, dangerously increased leverage; (b) knees bent more (ankles raised on block), pelvis level, spine more stable*

SPECIFIC EXERCISES WITH WEIGHTS ● ● ● ● ● ● ● ● ● ● ● ●

SIDE BEND

▧ Starting position
Begin standing side-on to a pulley machine. Your feet should be shoulder width apart and facing forwards. Grip the handle of a low pulley unit in your left hand, taking up any slack in the machine cord. Maintain an optimal posture.

▧ Action
Side bend your trunk to the right, reaching down the side of your right leg to try to touch the outside of your knee. Pause and then slowly lower the weight to stand upright again.

▧ Points to note
Make sure that you do not lean forwards or backwards as you perform the side bend. Keep your shoulders and hips square throughout the movement, and do not allow your knees to bend.

▧ Training tip
Focus your attention on the side of your trunk just above the hip. Do not swing the action; bend under control.

KNEE ROLLING

Starting position
Begin lying on your back with one knee bent. Attach a sling from a low pulley machine around your bent knee. Place your arms out in a 'T' shape to aid stability.

Action
Perform the knee rolling action, lowering your bent knee to the ground away from the pulley. As you do this the weight will lift. Pause and then bring your knee back to the upright position again by lowering the weight.

Points to note
The weight must move under control throughout the movement. Do not allow the weight to pull you. Once you have performed ten repetitions to one side, change your position to face the other way and perform ten repetitions to this side.

Training tip
If you find the sling from the weight pulley digs into your knee, wrap a towel around your knee beneath the sling before you start.

TRUNK FLEXION FROM HIGH PULLEY

▨ Starting position
Begin sitting astride a bench with your hands behind your neck. Grip the handle of a high pulley unit in both hands, behind your neck.

▨ Action
Flex your trunk, bending it without leaning forwards to lift the weight. Pause and then lower the weight by straightening your trunk again.

▨ Points to note
The action must be one of trunk bending, not bending from the hips.

▨ Training tip
Try to imagine you are aiming to touch your nose to your waist, rather than your nose to your knees. The direction of movement must be down, not forwards.

SIDE BEND FROM ABDOMINAL BENCH

Starting position
Lie on your side on a flat sit-up bench. Hook your feet under the pads, with your upper leg forwards, and lower leg back. Fold your lower arm across your chest and grip your upper shoulder with your hand. Reach along the side of your upper leg with your upper arm.

Action
Perform a side bend action, trying to lift your lower shoulder off the bench. Pause and then slowly lower to the starting position.

Points to note
You may only be able to lift your shoulder by 2–4 in (5 10 cm). Keep the action strictly to a side bend. Do not lean forwards or backwards.

Training tip
Keep looking forwards as you lift your shoulders, and try to reach your upper hand down towards the side of your upper leg.

SPINAL EXTENSION HOLD

▨ Starting position
Begin lying across a gym bench in the press-up position, with a training partner holding your feet down.

▨ Action
Perform the abdominal hollowing action to keep your spine in its neutral position. Holding this posture, firstly raise one arm to your side and then both arms. Hold the position and then place your hands back on the ground to rest.

▨ Points to note
You must keep your spine straight throughout this exercise; do not allow it to sag. Do not hold your breath; breathe normally.

▨ Training tip
Try to reach horizontally with the crown of your head, and 'lengthen the spine' as you perform the action. Build up the time you can hold the movement until you can hold the correct body position for 30 seconds.

STRETCHING ●

We have seen that one of the functions of the programme is to hold the spine stable in its neutral position. We can use this fact to aid us when practising stretching exercises of the muscles which attach to the pelvis. When the stretch is applied, the muscles pull on the pelvis, tending to move it. The F.L.A.T. muscles try to prevent movement by creating a stable base.

When stretching, the stretch should be performed slowly and held for 20–30 seconds. On no account use bouncing movements as these may damage the spine. Breathe out as the stretch is put on to help you relax tight muscles.

HIP FLEXOR STRETCH

Begin kneeling on one knee with the other leg bent to 90°, foot flat on the floor ('half kneeling'). Place your hand on a chair for support. *Tighten the abdominal muscles* and lunge forwards, causing the back leg to move into extension, and the hip flexor muscles to stretch. If the pelvis remains level, in its neutral position, the back leg will only move to the near vertical. However, if the abdominal muscles relax, the pelvis will tilt and the curve in the lower spine will increase. Now the leg moves back further, not because the hip flexor muscles are being stretched, but because the spine is moving excessively.

HAMSTRING STRETCH IN SITTING

We have seen earlier that the hamstrings are intimately linked to the depth of the curve in the lower back through their direct pull on the pelvis. When sitting, tight hamstrings will tilt the pelvis backwards, rounding the lower back and making back pain more likely. We can take advantage of this fact to exercise the F.L.A.T. muscles and improve sitting posture.

The exercise begins sitting on a low stool, with the knees bent. Sit tall, allowing the lower spine to hollow naturally. Tighten the abdominal muscles using the abdominal hollowing procedure and keep the pelvis level, in the neutral position. Maintaining this correct posture, slowly straighten one leg, feeling the tightness behind the knee. As soon as you feel the pelvis beginning to tilt, you have gone too far. Release the stretch slightly by bending the knee marginally to correct your posture. Maintain the stretch for 20–30 seconds.

ADDUCTOR STRETCH IN LYING

The principles underlying this stretch are similar to those described for the hamstring stretch. If the adductors are tight, when they are stretched they will pull on the pelvis and tilt it, tending to increase the lumbar curve. By using the F.L.A.T. muscles to maintain an optimal posture, we lessen the likelihood of injury.

Begin the adductor stretch by lying on the floor with the knees bent and feet flat. Perform the abdominal hollowing action to fix the pelvis. Keep the feet together, and allow the knees to slowly lower sideways to the floor. As soon as you feel the pelvis tilting, stop the exercise and raise the knees to correct your posture. Hold this new position for 20–30 seconds.

RECTUS FEMORIS STRETCH IN STANDING

Rectus femoris is a thigh muscle which straightens the knee, but also bends the hip. It is the muscle which is used in kicking, and one which is often damaged by soccer players. Stretching it is important, but performed incorrectly the stretch can place excessive stress on the lower back. By applying the F.L.A.T. principles the exercise is made both safer and far more effective.

Begin standing up straight, holding on to a wall for support. Perform the abdominal hollowing procedure to fix the pelvis. Bend one knee and reach back to take hold of your ankle. Keeping the pelvis level, pull the thigh backwards and at the same time try to bend your knee to touch your heel to your buttock. As soon as you feel your pelvis tilt, release the stretch slightly and correct your posture. Maintain the stretch for 20–30 seconds.

● ● ● ● ● ● ● ● ● ● ● ● ● ● ● ● **KEYPOINT** ● ● ● ● ● ● ● ● ● ● ● ● ● ● ● ●
Abdominal hollowing is used before the stretch is applied in each exercise. Keep the tummy pulled in tight to protect your lower back.

Sport specific exercises ● ● ● ● ● ● ● ● ● ● ● ● ● ● ● ●

Many movements in sport are performed rapidly, requiring power and speed. To be specific, the abdominal muscles must be trained to match this power requirement. Because these exercises move the spine quickly, they could be potentially dangerous if performed incorrectly. *To lessen the likelihood of injury, you must be able to perform all the exercises correctly for at least ten repetitions before you attempt the sport specific training.*

Rapid actions develop speed; rapid actions performed using weight resistance develop power. Each movement should be performed in a specific sequence to gradually build up intensity. Initially the movements should be slow and controlled until the exercise technique is perfected. Later, the speed of movement is gradually built up without resistance. Only when the action can be performed rapidly but in a precise, controlled, fashion should resistance be added. Resistance can increase when the exercises no longer feel challenging. Only light resistances should be used, as heavy weights will slow down the movement and reduce the training effect on power and speed.

MEDICINE BALL CURL-UP

Begin the exercise lying on your back on a mat with your knees bent, feet flat but not fixed. Your feet and knees should be wide apart – 20 in (50 cm). Make sure you can perform ten repetitions of the trunk curl exercise. Next, perform the action with a light (6 lb / 3 kg) medicine ball. As you come forwards, throw the ball between your knees to a training partner. Your partner catches the ball and throws it back to you. Catch it in the high position of the exercise and then lower yourself to the floor. Keep your abdominal muscles tight throughout the exercise.

MEDICINE BALL TWIST PASSING

Begin standing back-to-back with a training partner, about 10 in (25 cm) apart. You should both have your feet shoulder width apart, standing tall, holding your abdominal muscles in tight. Hold a medicine ball in both hands and twist round to the right. Your partner twists to the left, takes the medicine ball and then passes it back to you to their right. The movement should be continuous, like two cog wheels working together. Make sure you do not lean back as the movement speeds up.

To increase the overload of the exercise stand further apart and throw the medicine ball using the power of the trunk-twisting action to propel it rather than the arms. Keep the elbows tucked into your sides throughout the movement to reduce the work from the shoulders.

OVERHEAD THROW-IN

This movement is similar to a soccer throw-in. Stand facing a wall with one foot in front of the other. Hold a 6 lb (3 kg) medicine ball in both hands. Lift the ball overhead and extend the spine, keeping the abdominal muscles held in tight. (Be cautious not to overextend the spine; the movement should feel comfortable at all times.) Straighten and then slightly flex the spine to throw the ball at the wall. As the ball bounces off, catch it and control its descent by slightly arching the spine again. Repeat the action.

This exercise makes the abdominal muscles work hard to hold the spine stable and prevent it overextending as the ball is thrown and caught. However, excessive movement of the lower spine must be avoided.

PUNCHBAG SIDE BEND

Begin the exercise standing side-on to a punchbag. Your feet should be shoulder width apart, and your right arm should be straightened sideways to just touch the punchbag. Tighten your abdominal muscles and stand tall. Keep your arm straight, and side bend to the right to push the punchbag. As the bag swings back, control your return to an upright body position. Perform ten repetitions and then turn around so that your left arm touches the punch bag and you side bend to the left.

EXERCISE TO MUSIC

The F.L.A.T. principles can be applied to exercise to music (E.T.M.) classes of various types. The aim is to maintain an optimal posture, especially when fatigue sets in towards the end of the class, and to control pelvic angulation when performing other exercises.

During step aerobics, there is a tendency to allow the pelvis to tilt sideways when taking weight on to the stepping foot (*see* fig. 41). This occurs because the hip muscles and abdominal muscles at the side allow the pelvis to sag. As you take your weight on to your foot, stretch the spine and stand tall. Keep your pelvis level but tighten your abdominal muscles, and ensure that your knee is correctly positioned over the centre of your foot.

Many of the trunk exercises used in E.T.M. classes are performed to very high repetitions. As fatigue sets in there is a tendency for quality of exercise technique to suffer. Make sure that you are aware of the angle of your pelvis throughout the exercise bout. Do not allow your spine to extend excessively or maintain a flexed posture for any length of time. Try to keep your pelvis in the neutral position.

Fig.41 Posture during step aerobics: (a) incorrect – pelvis dips, spine leans over, knees have come together; (b) correct – pelvis level, spine lengthened, knees turned out slightly

EXERCISE IN WATER

The principles underlying the F.L.A.T. programme make it suitable for use in water. Water has a number of advantages for exercise involving the spine. The warmth of water is soothing, making it very useful following back pain, for example. In addition, water will support the body, taking some of the bodyweight off the joints and spine and so reducing pain. The muscles responsible for maintaining posture need to work less in water because your posture is supported by the water itself.

For the elderly, who may have circulatory problems as well as back pain, water has a further advantage. The pressure variation from the bottom of the pool to the surface actually helps the blood to return to the heart from the legs and so reduces 'tired legs'. Furthermore, the pressure changes created by the depth of the water assist in the reduction in blood pooling (blue veins in the legs) and swelling around the ankles.

PRINCIPLES OF WATER EXERCISE

BUOYANCY

Buoyancy is the degree to which your body will float when it is in water. Your individual buoyancy is determined by your body make-up. Bodyfat will make you more buoyant, while muscle makes you less. Plump individuals will tend to float, therefore, while those who are skinny are more likely to sink. If you have a large amount of muscle you may find it difficult to keep your legs afloat, so you will need assistance from floats when performing some leg exercises. The depth of the water you are standing in will also affect your buoyancy. The body will float more when it is in deeper water. When the water is waist high, your bodyweight is actually reduced by about 50%. When the water is up to your shoulders, your bodyweight is effectively reduced by 90%, so there is considerably less shock on the joints and spine in deeper water. However, because you float more in deeper water, movement can be harder to control, so be cautious.

Buoyancy can be used to support parts of the body, and to both
assist and resist movements. In fig. 42a, the subject is lying flat
in the water, holding on to the siderail of the swimming pool. To
enable them to float they have placed a rubber ring around their
waist, and a smaller ring around their legs. The rings can be
inflated or deflated according to the subject's buoyancy, to allow
the body to float either just beneath the surface of the water or
deeper. This supported lying position enables a selection of
spinal exercises to be performed with the body moving freely in
several directions.

Fig.42 *Buoyancy: (a) flotation aids; (b) buoyancy assistance;
(c) buoyancy resistance*

In fig. 42b, buoyancy is being used for assistance. The subject is performing a knee lift movement, but the legs are too heavy to perform the movement correctly. A ring has been placed around the knees to allow the legs to partially float, in effect making them lighter and assisting the upward action of the legs. In fig. 42c, the reverse situation is occurring. The exercise is hip extension, pressing the leg downwards. Now, the buoyancy of the rubber ring tending to lift the leg upwards is acting as a resistance to the downwards movement of the leg.

• • • • • • • • • • • • • • • **KEYPOINT** • • • • • • • • • • • • • • • • •
Buoyancy can be used to assist or resist a movement, and to support a bodypart during exercise.

RESISTANCE

Resistance is also provided by the movement of an object through water. The greater the amount of water which has to move, and the faster the object moves, the greater the resistance. Placing the hand side-on (*see* fig. 43a) and moving it slowly through the water provides a certain resistance to the arm muscles performing the movement. If the hand is turned through 90° so that it faces vertically (*see* fig. 43b), it provides considerably more resistance to movement and so the arm muscles must work harder. Speeding up the movement increases the work load still further.

To further boost muscle work we can use apparatus to increase resistance (*see* fig. 43c). Floats placed on their sides and webbed hand gloves are both useful to enhance a water workout.

a. **b.** **c.**

Fig.43 Using water resistance: (a) hand parallel to the water surface – little resistance; (b) hand perpendicular to the water surface – greater resistance; (c) using a float standing on its end – maximum resistance

Because fast movements offer greater resistance, rapid limb movements are useful when working on trunk stability. Standing in deep water and pushing a float rapidly forwards and backwards, for example, will tend to displace the trunk. Tightening the abdominal muscles against this displacement enhances trunk stability.

●●●●●●●●●●●●●●●●● *KEYPOINT* ●●●●●●●●●●●●●●●●●
Less streamlined objects offer greater water resistance, and can be used to make an exercise harder.

SAFETY CONSIDERATIONS

Obviously water is a dangerous medium to work in, but these dangers can be considerably reduced by taking sensible precautions. Poor swimmers should never practise water exercises in water above waist height, and they must stay close to the poolside at all times. Young children must be continuously supervised, however strong their swimming may appear.

When using apparatus to float, it is easy to become disorientated, and panic. For this reason, always exercise with a partner. When one of you is working, the other should be standing by, offering support and encouragement.

Many accidents occur when moving to and from the pool, so *walk* on wet surfaces, don't run. Also, when getting into and out of the pool, be cautious, and use the steps rather than jumping or diving in, especially with shallow water.

●●●●●●●●●●●●●●●●● *KEYPOINT* ●●●●●●●●●●●●●●●●●
In water, it's always safety first.

WATER EXERCISES •

TRUNK SIDE BENDING

Begin the exercise lying on your back in the water, holding on to the siderail of the pool (*see* fig. 44a). Choose a wide grip, and keep your arms locked. Ask your training partner to place a rubber ring around your waist, and a smaller (or less inflated) ring around your shins. The rings should be inflated sufficiently to allow your body to float just beneath the surface of the water.

Keep your legs straight and move them from side to side in the water to make your trunk side-flex. Keep the action slow and controlled, and pause as you reach the end point of each sideways movement.

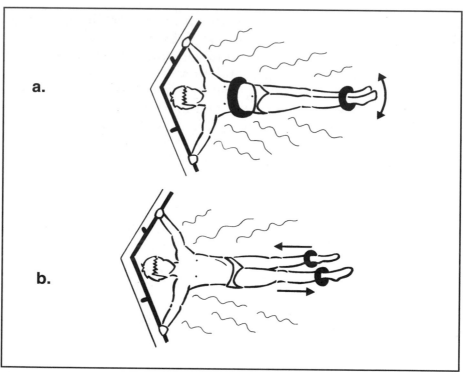

Fig.44 *Water exercises: (a) trunk side bending; (b) leg shortening and lengthening*

LEG SHORTENING AND LENGTHENING

Begin the exercise lying on your back in the water, holding on to the siderail of the pool (*see* fig. 44b). Choose a wide grip, and keep your arms locked. Ask your training partner to place a rubber ring around your waist, and an armband on each leg. The rings should be inflated sufficiently to allow your body to float just beneath the surface of the water. (Some subjects may not require a ring around the waist.)

Keep your body in line, and shorten one leg while lengthening the other, so that your pelvis tilts sideways. Do not allow your spine to flex or extend; isolate the movement to the pelvis.

LEG LIFT

Hold on to the siderail of the pool above head height. Keep your back flat against the poolside (*see* fig. 44c). Lift and lower your legs, keeping them straight, and tighten your abdominal muscles using the abdominal hollowing procedure. If you find this movement difficult, place a rubber ring around your legs to assist the lifting motion. If the movement seems very easy, perform the action more quickly to increase the resistance.

Fig.44 (c) *Leg lift;* **(d)** *resisted trunk rotation*

RESISTED TRUNK ROTATION

Begin the exercise standing in chest deep water within reach of the poolside (*see* fig. 44d). Place your feet shoulder width apart and stand tall, pulling your tummy in. Stretch your arms out to the side, keeping them just below the surface of the water. Your hands should be flat at 90° to the surface of the water, fingers together.

Twist your trunk, without bending forwards or backwards. Twist round as far as is comfortable, but do not force the movement. If you find the exercise easy, either wear webbed gloves, or hold a float in each hand positioned at 90° to the water surface to increase resistance. Speeding up the movement will also make the exercise harder, but make sure that you maintain a good posture.

KNEE TWIST

Begin the exercise with your back on the poolside, gripping the siderail with outstretched arms (*see* fig. 44e). Bend one knee and place a rubber ring around the knee of this leg. Tighten your abdominal muscles and flatten the small of your back towards the poolside. Keeping the tummy tight, twist the trunk to bring the bent knee across the body and on to the side of the pool. Perform five repetitions to one side, then change legs and perform five repetitions to the other side.

BODY CURL

Lie on your front, and grip the siderail of the pool (*see* fig. 44f). Bend the legs and trunk to bring your knees towards your chest, and your feet on to the poolside. Pause, and then stretch the body out straight again. The movement becomes harder if a float is placed around the feet, as buoyancy resists the leg movement under the surface of the water.

e.　　　　f.

Fig.44 (e) Knee twist; (f) body curl

INDEX